FIVE FOR FREEDOM

LUCRETIA MOTT

ELIZABETH CADY STANTON

LUCY STONE

SUSAN B. ANTHONY

CARRIE CHAPMAN CATT

Lucretia Mott

Elizabeth Cady Stanton

Lucy Stone

Susan B. Anthony

Carrie Chapman Catt

FIVE
FOR
FREEDOM

by Constance Buel Burnett

*With a great sum
obtained I this freedom*
ACTS 23:28

GREENWOOD PRESS, PUBLISHERS
WESTPORT, CONNECTICUT

The Library of Congress cataloged this book as follows:

920.72
BUR

Burnett, Constance (Buel)
  Five for freedom; Lucretia Mott, Elizabeth Cady Stanton,
Lucy Stone, Susan B. Anthony, Carrie Chapman Catt.
New York, Greenwood Press, 1968 [ᶜ1953]

  317, [3] p. 23 cm.

  Bibliography: p. [319]–[320]

  1. Woman—Rights of women. 2. Women in the U. S.—Biog.
I. Title.

HQ1412.B8   1968   301.41′2′0922   68–8734

Library of Congress   [3]

To

the hundreds of women

who campaigned

with tireless energy

and courage

The Nineteenth Amendment

When Thomas Jefferson asserted that all democratic government derived its "just powers from the consent of the governed," neither he nor other members of the Continental Congress caught the full import of his words. Their next act was to withhold that right of consent from half the citizens of the republic they proposed to found. Not until a decade before the Civil War did the forgotten half start a revolt which eventually won them full citizenship.

Today, women have largely forgotten that bitterly fought crusade of almost a century's duration. Hardly a trace now remains of those practices and customs which barred women from all colleges, denied them a place in the professions, and refused them all but the lowest paid employment.

All over America, on Election Day in November, every housewife may exercise her right to choose the nation's lawmakers and accept or reject the laws that shall govern her. She might prize the vote more highly did she stop to reflect that as recently as 1920 she belonged to a disfranchised class —with criminals, illiterates and idiots. Of the legal injustices and social abuses which kept her sisters of earlier generations ignorant and subject, she has but a vague memory.

Woman's struggle for independence and the heroism of her pioneer leaders deserve wider commemoration. Because of their stubborn defense of her rights, she stands equipped at a crucial moment in history to share man's coming-of-age as a citizen of the world.

Born of the moral awakening to free the Negro, the Woman's Rights Movement in America began with the pathetic, courageous protest of a few crinoline-skirted abolitionists, chief of whom was Lucretia Mott, gifted Quaker preacher and native of Nantucket Island.

It was she who stirred young Elizabeth Cady Stanton to open rebellion. Not long afterwards, two high-spirited girls —Lucy Stone and Susan B. Anthony—aroused by wrongs they saw, pledged their lives to the crusade. These four might be truly called the Founding Mothers of civil, economic and social rights for women in the United States.

To Carrie Chapman Catt, the most notable of the leaders who followed them, belongs the distinction of having transformed a still struggling movement into a hard-hitting organization. The vast army of suffragists she headed was so doggedly persistent and so skilled in political methods that Congress could no longer ignore their demands.

Now that the right of free elections is at stake in many parts of the world, the story of these five women has become a timely one. Their difficulties and setbacks were little different from those of the free nations striving to agree on a course of action for the common good. In principle they were fervently united; in character, temperament, and opinions as to method, almost as fervently divided. But in spite of mistakes and dissensions, the great liberating principle they served marched on.

The story of these women is the story of Democracy, maturing, civilizing, and ennobling the race. It is a process of growth to which all free men and women are dedicated.

THE AUTHOR MAKES GRATEFUL ACKNOWLEDGMENT

To the Alice Stone Blackwell Fund Committee, for permission to use material covered by copyright in *Lucy Stone—Pioneer,* by Alice Blackwell.

To Harper & Brothers, for permission to quote from *Elizabeth Cady Stanton as Revealed in Her Letters, Diary and Reminiscences,* edited by Theodore Stanton and Harriot Stanton Blatch.

To Mrs. Norah Stanton Barney, for her generous co-operation in my search for source material about her grandmother.

To Alma Lutz, author of *Created Equal,* a biography of Elizabeth Cady Stanton, for her kind assistance in tracing the authenticity of a needed quotation.

To Mary Gray Peck, author of *Carrie Chapman Catt,* for her generous consent to my use of her book as basic source material for the article on Mrs. Catt, and for permission to quote.

To Muriel Fuller, for her enthusiastic interest and skillful performance as an editor.

CONTENTS

I

Lucretia Mott

"How shall I describe to you Lucretia Mott—the most brilliant eyes. Such a face and such regal erectness. No one else ever stood upright before!"

Thomas Wentworth Higginson

"Addison, in *The Spectator*, refers to a French author, who mentions that the ladies of the court of France, in his time, thought it ill-breeding and a kind of female pedantry, to pronounce a hard word right, for which reason they took frequent occasion to use hard words, that they might show a politeness in murdering them. The author further adds that a lady of some quality at court, having accidentally made use of a hard word in a proper place, and pronounced it right, the whole assembly was out of countenance with her."

The History of Woman Suffrage (Vol. I)

ONE

While the helpless, submissive female of eighteenth-century literature was still the popular ideal, a unique way of life was evolving in an obscure corner of the American Colonies, a very different type, which was to foreshadow the twentieth-century woman.

The island of Nantucket, isolated by thirty miles of sea from the customs and traditions of the mainland, was, as early as 1700, under the virtual rule of a woman. In intellect and ability Mary Coffin Starbuck so towered above the rest of the settlement that she became its acknowledged leader. Without the advice or sanction of the "Great Woman," as the islanders called her, Nantucket Elders made no important decisions.

Although she was the most influential person on the island, Mary Starbuck never omitted that deference toward the opposite sex which, in those days, was so excellent a virtue in a female—especially one admitted to male councils. Actually, she ran the Town Meetings, but always discreetly, behind such phrases as "My husband thinks" or "Nathaniel and I feel," and this amiable policy, not sufficiently cultivated by strong-minded wives, earned her a long and uninterrupted public career.

It availed her nothing, however, against the strict Presbyterian rule, then prevailing in Nantucket, which forbade even the "Great Woman" to open her mouth in church. Here Providence itself intervened in the shape of a visiting Quaker, sent from England on a mission to the island.

Quaker methods of worship not only granted women a share in church government, but elected them to the ministry. This must have impressed Mary Starbuck. At all events, she very soon announced in Town Meeting that the "inner light" had spoken unmistakably to Nathaniel and herself, urging them to join the Society of Friends. Thereupon a good majority of the other islanders heard the same voice and left the Presbyterian fold.

That a religion acknowledging the equality of men and women should have found its way to the remote spot where Mary Starbuck lived seems consistent. It came perhaps in answer to her prayer for a more enlightened faith, and certainly in answer to the needs of a community where the female population was already beginning to outnumber the male.

For, from the moment they saw the native Indians launch their canoes through the surf for the chase and capture of an offshore whale, Nantucket men were seduced by the exhilarating risks and sometimes fabulous rewards of a dangerous calling. They became the most expert whalemen in the world, second to none in daring and physical prowess, and their women were of the same hardy breed.

Fathers, sons, lovers sailed off with the whaling ships and were gone for years at a time, some never to be seen again.

Women, as they can when they must, took on the burdens of men. Tall myths are still circulated of the athletic feats of Nantucket women. One hefty goodwife is reported to have picked up an oxcart blocking her path; another could throw a man as easily as she tossed a beanbag. These stalwart ladies of early Nantucket thought nothing of strolling seven miles and back, to a neighbor on the other side of the island, for a dish of tea. The man of the house was sea leagues away, and who was there to upset the shining order of their homes or dispute their right to gossip as often and as late as they chose?

Left in charge of family resources, women controlled the island economy. Into their hands fell most of the wealth brought back by the whaling fleets and India trade. So profitable were some of these voyages and so thriftily did affairs prosper, while the men were away, that it became the avowed aim of Nantucket housewives to keep "a clean hearth and a husband at sea."

While whaling was at its height, Nantucket held an unbeatable record in the industry and uniqueness of its women. Three illustrious Americans have been able to boast Nantucket mothers: Benjamin Franklin; Maria Mitchell, the astronomer; and Lucretia Mott, a collateral descendant of the "Great Woman." It has been claimed for Lucretia Mott that she was the most enlightened woman of her period. To her influence may be largely credited the start of an organized movement for woman's rights in America.

Born in Nantucket in 1793, Lucretia's childhood was colored by seagoing traditions. Her father, Captain Thomas Coffin, was in the East India trade and his wife, Anna, supported the family during his absences with the energy and competence for which island wives were famous.

Lucretia was not the oldest child, but she was the cleverest and most responsible, so it was she whom Anna left in charge of the house when she went on her periodic trips to the "Continent"—Nantucket term for Cape Cod—where she traded whale oil, sperm candles, and India goods for needles and thread, matches, and other necessities the island did not yield.

Anna must have cautioned Lucretia firmly to keep the other children out of the small front room next to the parlor, in which she kept shop. On its shelves were stored sealed packages of India and China tea, jars of ginger, spices, ivory and jade curios, chinaware, lengths of nankeen and bolts of silk. In contrast to the meagerness and austerity of their island life these small home shops must have opened the door of romance for many a Nantucket child.

The strictest economy was practiced on the island, dependent for its supplies on the uncertainties of ships and weather. Imported luxuries were for sale, not for consumption. Sailor's fare—fish, salt pork and corned beef—was also Nantucket fare, healthy but monotonous, even though housewives developed a wizardry of their own with chowders. Lucretia knew no greater reward for an extra stint of knitting than to be allowed to roast a potato in the immense kitchen fireplace in the cellar.

"Mind thee takes the smallest," was Anna Coffin's reminder, for potatoes were a treat reserved for Quaker "first days" and "veal feasts," those rare banquets which celebrated the arrival of fresh meat on the island.

But no matter what the state of the larder, visitors were always welcome, especially since conditions made it impossible to entertain lavishly. Nantucket hospitality was proverbial—and so was the chowder! "Put in six more potatoes," the word relayed hastily to the kitchen, when unexpected guests arrived, was a household joke. The easy custom of sharing what was on the table, as well as the dignity of her Quaker breeding, made a great hostess of Lucretia Mott later on, when her home became the rallying center for the liberals of her day.

Another Nantucket custom which contributed to her education, was the foregathering of friends of all ages in a large circle around the evening fire for "conversations." The child Lucretia sat mouse-still on her small ladder-back chair, her unwinking gaze and flushed face indicating how intently she followed the adult talk.

Like all Quaker children, she had been taught to heed the "inner monitor," to cultivate a listening and obedient heart. Quaker meetings were not devoted to ritual, but to quietness and earnest self-examination. This training deepened and enriched an already gifted young intellect and disciplined an impetuous little girl.

The stupidity of others made her temper flare. They called her spitfire in school and at home, but easily forgave her spurts of anger. They were brief and impulsively regretted. She remained lovable all her life, working hard to improve herself and putting into the effort an amount of enthusiasm that was disarming.

When she was seven she had an unforgettable experience, but one not uncommon to Nantucket children. Her father, three years gone on a voyage round the Horn, was not heard from for a full twelve months, and was given up as lost. Then one day the quiet of Nantucket village was broken by the shouts of the town crier. From corner to street corner the news traveled. It was a summons to the townfolk that a ship had been sighted from the windmill on the island's highest point. Nearer and nearer the Coffin home sounded the call, and Anna, hearing it, stood motionless in her kitchen.

Her husband's ship, the *Trial*, was too large to cross the Nantucket Bar. Her home port was Woods Hole, but if Captain Coffin was alive, he would fly signals from his masthead and sail close enough to the island to be recognized.

"Quick, Lucretia, the spyglass!"

Up two flights of stairs to the "walk," the lookout on every Nantucket roof, the mother hurried, with the children breathlessly excited at her heels. Lucretia held the precious spyglass carefully in both hands.

Anna's shaking fingers found it hard to unfasten the trapdoor at the top of the attic ladder. At last the hook yielded and the family stepped out on the railed-in platform. About them the whole town was on the rooftops, training their telescopes on the eastern horizon.

While the children tugged at her skirts, impatient for their turn at the glass, Anna looked long and hard before she admitted bitter disappointment, as she had time and again these past three years. Nantucket wives knew rigging as they knew the patterns woven on their looms. This was not her husband's ship.

It was customary for the townfolk to drop their work and greet a home-coming ship. This day everyone went down to the wharves but Anna Coffin. The hours dragged inside her house. She drove herself from one task to another—shut the windows hastily when muffled cheering came from the harbor, started to cook an early supper.

And then without warning the front door burst open, as though blown in by a great wind. "Anna!" The familiar call, ringing through the house again, stopped her heart.

When a man stepped alive like that out of three years' absence and a year's silence, Nantucket women stood the shock of relief as stoically as they endured grief. Anna Coffin did not even drop the skillet she was holding, but Lucretia never forgot the look on her mother's face as she turned to welcome Thomas back.

Captain Coffin did not go to sea again. The *Trial* and her cargo had been confiscated off the coast of South America for alleged violation of neutrality, and, after a long stay in Valparaiso, vainly trying to obtain redress from the Spanish courts, he had to trek across the Andes and book passage home from Brazil. He had had his fill of unlucky voyages. This one had meant the loss of his ship. Not many months after his return he affiliated himself with a merchant in Boston and the family left Nantucket, but not before the island had placed its indelible stamp on Lucretia.

Unique island expressions, social customs and household crafts were all of Nantucket that remained to her, and she clung to them. Her children to the third generation were taught the "Nantucket way" and, to the end of Lucretia's life, nautical lore flavored her conversation. She even added weather comments to the dates of some of her letters, terse and exact as the log of a ship's master.

TWO

On the mainland, Thomas and Anna Coffin stuck to their Nantucket habits of independence. Lucretia's father, a firm believer in democratic ways, at first sent his children to the Boston public schools instead of to the Quaker school.

The term "select Quaker school" was offensive to him. He wanted no snobbery in his children. However, he soon discovered that Massachusetts taxpayers differed from Quakers in one respect. They were unwilling to spend money on their daughters' education. Girls were allowed to use the public schools for only two hours each afternoon, after the boys had left, and high schools for girls were unheard of.

Lucretia was therefore sent back to the Quakers for the last two years of her school life. By that time she was already a good mixer who had rubbed shoulders with the poor of a big city.

At the Quaker Seminary in Nine Partners, New York, she first heard slavery debated as a great social evil. On this issue, however, her own family and most of the Quakers she knew were conservatives, although a few public-spirited Quakers were joining a movement to boycott sugar, cotton, and all

kinds of merchandise that were produced by slave labor.
Thus, she came early face to face with the controversy
which was to split the Quaker sect into two factions and
make of her a great revolutionary. But for the moment she
was only thirteen. Injustices at Nine Partners School loomed
larger. She reacted to them with the audacity she was to
show all her life.

School punishments were often too severe and some teachers misused their authority. When one of the boys was sentenced to prison fare and solitary confinement in a closet for
a minor offense, Lucretia defied the inflexible rule of Quaker
segregation, slipped into the strictly forbidden area where
the boys lived and passed food under the culprit's door.

In her fifteenth year, Lucretia went back to Nine Partners
as an assistant teacher and made two discoveries which greatly
astounded a new and naïve member of the faculty. Even in
a Quaker school, girl students paid as much as the boys for
tuition, but received less education. Moreover as a woman
instructor, she was paid only half the salary a man got.

Too young to remedy the injustice, she still had spunk
enough to reject the idea that women were inferior. "I resolved," she said of those early years, "to claim for myself,
all that an impartial Creator had bestowed."

Among the faculty at Nine Partners was the tall, shy boy
who was to become her husband. James Mott had the gentleness which belongs sometimes to big men. His flaxen hair,
cut Quaker fashion, framed a kindly, rather stubborn young
face. He was painfully taciturn and so tongue-tied in the
classroom that he soon made up his mind to earn his livelihood some other way.

The new little assistant teacher, whose bonnet scarcely reached to his shoulder and whose black eyes sparkled with more fun than was altogether proper in a Quaker, was a dynamo of energy, initiative and fluent conversation. She was quick to recognize quality in the bashful young master who worshiped her at a distance. Diffident James was drawn out of his reserve in spite of himself, especially when he discovered underneath her gaiety a girl as devoutly religious as himself. That her lover was a shy man made his love-making more disarming and sincere. Ardent wooing might never have won Lucretia. She had a shrewd ear and a keen eye for honesty.

James and Lucretia were married when he was twenty-three and she but eighteen. They were to remain unlike in almost everything except their valorous convictions, which were dangerously liberal for those days. Even there Lucretia crusaded with a dash inherited perhaps from her seafaring ancestry while James weighed the cost of every stand he took, and then held it with unshaken calm.

Hard times, brought on by the war of 1812, interfered at first with the prospects of the young couple. Business everywhere was slow, and James, conscientious and methodical, tried one opening after another with little success. For a while they were forced to live under the same roof with Lucretia's family. Finally, when commerce revived, James was offered a position with a reliable cotton merchant in Philadelphia. He had two children to support now and was too hard pressed to quibble over the meagerness of his first year's pay.

Lucretia, however, was soon able to augment the family income. After a long spell of domestic cares her mind hungered for use. Teaching was the one profession permitted to women in those days and she had served her apprenticeship at Nine Partners. What more natural than to go back to the work in which she had been successful?

She secured the patronage of a few Philadelphia Friends, engaged a cousin to help her, and considered the school well launched with four pupils. So it proved. Inside of seven months the four had increased to forty.

It was well that the project once started could not be dropped and that its demands filled her days to overflowing, for a stunning blow struck the young mother at this time in the sudden death of her little boy. He had been a happy, lovable child, specially dear to everyone. Lucretia fought heartbreak in the self-reliant Quaker way, searching deep within herself for a renewal of faith. She found it comforted her to stand up in Meeting and share with others the fruits of her quest.

Her eloquence attracted attention and soon thereafter, when she was only twenty-five, Lucretia's famous ministry began.

It is hard to believe there was ever a more youthful or captivating preacher. In her austere, full-skirted Quaker costume, she looked childlike and frail, but she held herself like a queen. The modest organdy bonnet could not hide the regal brow nor the brilliantly penetrating eyes.

Lucretia was always to possess the power to fascinate. No matter how eminent the other speakers on a public platform, her small, erect figure soon became the focus of attention, and Heaven help the opponent who underestimated her size! Lucretia Mott became a lioness as soon as her principles were attacked.

Her election as a minister followed the usual Quaker rule. There were no trained or professional preachers. Congregations sat in meditative silence till one of their number felt impelled by the Spirit to address the Meeting. Those manifesting a "gift in the ministry" might be recommended at a quarterly meeting of Church Elders. If approved, they became official ministers who went from place to place, preaching without pay. Sermons were not prepared. It was a Quaker rule to rely on inspiration, and out of this habit grew Lucretia's ability to think on her feet and to speak fearlessly.

Her appointment as minister coincided happily with a raise in salary for James, enabling her to withdraw from the now prosperous school and devote herself more to her own children and the study her ministry required.

The next ten years were years of quiet maturing. She accepted no invitations to preach outside Philadelphia during this period. Five young children made it difficult to leave home. However, Lucretia never allowed domestic concerns to interfere with that enthralling adventure with books she sedately referred to as "the improvement of the mind."

Her keen intellect demanded real fare. "The ladies' department in the periodicals of the day had no attraction for me," is Lucretia's single comment on the sentimental twaddle fed her generation.

While she nursed her youngest child, the big four-poster bed made a convenient table for the massive works of William Penn, the great Quaker leader. These she studied so thoroughly that years later she could quote accurately from them, to the confusion of Quaker opponents. For from the beginning of her ministry, Lucretia began to alarm conservative

Friends. She boldly declared herself in favor of the abolition of slavery and of the liberal preachments of Elias Hicks.

The differences between orthodox and liberal Quakers were fast approaching a climax. They disagreed about whether or not they should oppose slavery, and, if so, to what lengths. They quarreled over interpretations of the Scriptures and rules in regard to speech and dress. They even fought about the prescribed shade of gray and brown they should wear.

Lucretia deplored doctrinal squabbling. She obeyed trivial rules and regulations rather than fuss over small issues. But when bigotry and self-interest blinded her Quaker brethren to principles of equality and freedom, she forged ahead without them. Thus she fought for the great humanitarian causes of her period shoulder to shoulder with "the world's people," since her own seemed temporarily preoccupied in fighting among themselves.

THREE

All this while, she and James had been wrestling with a decision which neither of them could evade any longer. Their present income, modest but sufficient, was derived from the prosperous cotton industry which employed slave labor. Was it not inconsistent, and worse, to benefit from a system they both abhorred?

Intrepid always, Lucretia was ready before James to take the only honest step and its hard consequences. Bitter memories of the first years of marriage, when he was unable to earn an adequate living for his family, made the decision anguishing for him. She understood, and did not urge him. When, finally, he did start all over again, in the wool industry, untainted by slavery, they both held their heads higher in spite of near poverty.

Shortly after this, the more liberal Quakers—the followers of Elias Hicks—separated themselves from the main body of the sect. Now it was James who made up his mind before Lucretia. Distressed by the division in Quaker ranks and always willing to yield a merely doctrinal point in the interests of unity, she hesitated. However, she felt Elias Hicks was reviving the true spirit of Quakerism. His ideas' were nearest her own free and enlightened thinking, and so she left the orthodox camp and joined James in becoming "a Hicksite."

It was from now on that she earned the epithet "fighting Quaker," bestowed on all Friends who forsook a purely neutral attitude. The loss of old friends when she resigned from the conservative camp was only the beginning of Quaker persecution because of her abolition work. As time passed, she was more and more convinced that she must preach immediate emancipation of the Negro.

Many Friends argued piously that gradual liberation would be better for the Negro himself and that her militant preaching was contrary to peaceful Quaker methods. They did not add that quick emancipation would strike a blow at comfortable Quaker incomes. Lucretia, having had to face that painful dilemma herself, knew what was behind their reluctance. She went on preaching as her conscience dictated.

The imprisonment of William Lloyd Garrison following his denunciation of a Baltimore slave trader marked the beginning of her affiliation with abolitionists outside the Quaker fold. When Garrison was released from jail, James and Lucretia were the only ones to offer him the shelter of their home.

Three years later, Garrison, the poet Whittier and a few other abolition sympathizers called a convention in Philadelphia to organize the American Anti-Slavery Association. Both the Motts attended; James to become a charter member, Lucretia as a guest, and in recognition of her antislavery preaching in Quaker Meeting Houses.

To this conclave of men only three women besides herself

were invited. They were mute onlookers, except Lucretia, who made two unscheduled speeches.

It was unheard of in those days for women to address a gathering of men. But Lucretia, like her Nantucket forebear the "Great Woman," could turn on the necessary female modesty when required. Apologizing for what might be "regarded as an intrusion," she pointed out demurely that to "transpose" certain words in the Association's charter would make for greater clarity and emphasis. Her proposal was accepted with excessive gallantry. One young man, indeed, was so immensely impressed, he turned all the way around in his seat to stare at the woman who knew the meaning of the word "transpose," a revealing comment on the education of the female sex at that period!

Lucretia felt impelled to speak again. It happened, an hour later, that members of the Association were tempted to take a less valiant stand against slavery. A messenger arrived suddenly with letters from two prominent citizens of Philadelphia. They declined membership in the Association for reasons of prudence, and suggested a more cautious policy toward freeing the Negro. The advice held a hint of threat. Dismay and hesitation gripped the meeting until Lucretia, her small bonneted head bobbing up for the second time, remarked firmly: "Right principles are stronger than great names. If our principles are right, why should we be cowards?"

Why indeed? Applause, cries of "Hear! Hear!" and "Speech!" from stouthearted listeners, encouraged her to a short but fiery declaration of abolitionist tenets, while the ears of those who had spoken for retreat must have burned. Over James's sober, bespectacled face passed a flicker of amusement. He could have told the others they hadn't a chance in the world to recant—not with Lucretia there! To the unsuspecting men who competed with her on public platforms, he felt moved occasionally to offer a friendly tip. "If she thinks thee is wrong, thee had better look it over again," was his whispered warning to one eminent speaker, who sat down a trifle too complacently just before Lucretia took the floor.

Not many weeks after the formation of the men's American Anti-Slavery Association, the women who had been its guests, and some others in sympathy with its cause, banded together in a similar association. Lucretia served as President for many years. Her record of the Society's start has both humor and pathos. Women's clubs were unknown in those days, church bazaars and sewing circles being the only activities outside the home deemed proper for a lady. So when this group of women, the first to organize in the state of Pennsylvania, and perhaps in the Union, gathered together on this epoch-making occasion, not one of them had the faintest notion how to conduct a meeting.

Fortunately there was one person present competent to help them out of their dilemma, James McCrummel, a Negro spectator. They invited him to take the chair. And so, with the assistance of a member of the race they themselves were seeking to enlighten, the Philadelphia Female Anti-Slavery Society was organized.

By this time the two eldest of the Mott children were sufficiently grown to assume family responsibilities when Lucretia had to be absent. She now accepted full duties as a minister, occasionally leaving home on long trips, visiting Quaker

Societies in states close to Philadelphia and in her beloved Nantucket.

Travel by stagecoach was uncomfortable and tedious. Her energy on these pilgrimages almost outdid that of the stalwart James who sometimes accompanied her. In spite of a frail body she had the wiry endurance which often goes with an active and courageous temperament. Her fervor for unpopular causes placed her always at the hub of excitement and conflict, oblivious to personal danger. Lucky for James that his nerves were iron and his nature placid!

The single-minded zeal of a reformer, as well as her Quaker training, made her blind and deaf to all esthetic appeal. She had a sailor's habit of watching the sky, but it never occurred to her that there was anything to look at but the weather.

"It is beautiful, now thee points it out," she would admit when prodded into admiring a sunset, "but I should not have noticed it. I have always taken more interest in *human* nature."

A classic remark of hers on this score was reserved for a later trip to England when she visited Warwick, Kenilworth, and other places of historic interest and beauty. Missing perhaps the tactful promptings of her more discriminating family, Lucretia was heard to say with her usual candor, "I wish someone would tell me what to admire."

Her indifference to external things was one secret of her strength. What her eyes registered made little impression; what her moral sense affirmed she saw and believed. So constituted and fortified, she could be undisturbed in the midst of scenes of violence, and they were soon to occur with the growing opposition to abolitionists.

FOUR

Five years after the modest start of the Female Anti-Slavery Society of Philadelphia, it held a convention, fittingly enough in Pennsylvania Hall, a public building recently dedicated to "Liberty and the Rights of Man."

While the women, better versed now in parliamentary law, conducted their business within, a disorderly mob surrounded the hall for the purpose of breaking up the meeting. The din outside increased steadily as the crowd grew, but the convention ignored it. If any woman present was tempted to move adjournment, one look at the calm group on the platform where Angelina Grimké Weld, Lucretia Mott, Esther Moore, and one or two other hardy souls sat unmoved, quieted the impulse.

Meanwhile, finding every door barred and the windows locked, the hoodlums threatened to force an entrance. Continuous catcalls, shouting and demoniac yells were interrupted only by more ominous silences, which meant the crowd was preparing new deviltry.

The climax came with a crash of splintering glass as the first stone was hurled through a window. The mob stormed the building then, breaking pane after pane and throwing vitriol through the gaping holes into the auditorium. By that time the Society had finished its business for the day. In the midst of the pandemonium, Angelina and Lucretia encouraged and exhorted the others, urging them not to give up their stand for abolition, but to meet next day in a house offered by one of their members.

By some miracle, none of the women was hurt, either during the attack on the building, nor as they passed through the ugly crowd massed for blocks outside. Two or three hours after they vacated the hall, it went up in flames.

The rioting had only just begun. All that night Philadelphia was in an uproar. It was known that the Mayor of the city wished to put a stop to abolition activities. Police protection was nonexistent.

Warned by friends, James and Lucretia prepared that evening for an attack on their own house. Their preparations were characteristic. They sent the younger children with a few valuables next door, and sat down calmly in the parlor to await events.

A handful of friendly neighbors stood by to give what encouragement and cheer they could.

Young Thomas Mott went outside to scout and report the whereabouts of the rioters. Like any boy he reveled in the excitement until he heard the sound of many running feet and caught a note of savagery in the distant shouts. Panic gripped him as he ran back to warn his parents.

"They're coming," he choked breathlessly, slamming and bolting the front door behind him. Then, meeting his father's calm, fortifying gaze, he took a deep breath and walked quietly over to his mother's chair, his hands clenched and ready for use if necessary.

There was a period of tense waiting while the yells and commotion in the streets grew nearer. Thomas knew that, come what might, his father and mother would never yield to coercion. He knew also that tar and feathering was still the favorite reprisal of lawless gangs and that the house was almost certain to be set on fire.

But as the minutes passed, the noise outside seemed to abate and then fade in the distance. Wondering what could have diverted the mob, but alert for a surprise maneuver, they did not relax their vigil. One hour passed quietly, then two. Peace seemed to have settled on the neighborhood. It appeared safe at last to go to bed.

Next day James and Lucretia learned that a quick-witted friend had himself joined the rioters, when they were but a few blocks from the house. Brandishing a stick and shouting, "On to the Motts!" he headed them up a succession of wrong streets. The ruse so scattered and confused the crowd that they never reorganized.

But the burning of Pennsylvania Hall, with its terrifying sequel, was only one of many similar incidents faced by leaders of abolition. Lucretia's composure in the midst of rioting became a legend.

Respect was something Lucretia evoked unconsciously. Vilification she received in plenty, but in her work for the slave she was subjected to no personal indignities. Rotten eggs and tomatoes hurled by hoodlums in the audience were reserved for the Grimké sisters and other women abolitionists. It was the public speaking of Sarah and Angelina Grimké which first precipitated this sort of attack and roused the fanatical rage of the clergy.

Daughters of a wealthy Charleston slaveholder, the Grimkés were powerfully convincing crusaders, not only because of their close connection with the slave system, but because they were eyewitnesses to its cruelties. They started their missionary work almost timidly at first, as befitted members of a traditionally cloistered and diffident sex, pleading the Negro's cause in private homes to small groups of women only. But they were soon persuaded to join abolitionist ranks and spread their message fearlessly from town to town, wherever they could secure a church or hall.

Their drama and the obvious veracity of their report drew great numbers of men as well as women to their meetings and converted many to abolition. Most of the clergy of that period, however, were shocked by the spectacle of a woman speaking from a pulpit or platform and, above all, addressing a mixed audience.

No other conclusion could be drawn from this brazen conduct than that the Grimké sisters were courting masculine attention!

Moreover, what business had women interfering in an economic problem hitherto left to the judgment of men? If such an influence continued unchecked, the dependent, biddable creature, who was necessary to male comfort and self-esteem, might soon become extinct.

In a flurry of concern, the General Association of Congregational Ministers of Massachusetts issued a letter of protest, exhorting the clergy of all denominations to close their doors to that dangerous innovation, the woman speaker, and extolling the "clinging vine" as the true prototype of womanhood.

Lucretia's full share of abuse was not lacking, but it came chiefly from the Quakers, who were well used to seeing a woman address a gathering, and whose quarrel was rather with her abolitionist preaching and u   this score an attempt was made to "disow   e to disputes over the letter of religi   d not a rap, she was too smart to be t____

As though having to fight her own people was not enough, Lucretia soon found herself obliged to take sides in a quarrel within the Pennsylvania Anti-Slavery Society itself. Since its founding day, when she had been an impromptu speaker, the organization led by Garrison had voted to admit women to full and equal membership with men. But the move was violently opposed.

A large number of men, who were at odds about other matters in the Association as well, resigned and formed what they called the "New Organization."

Zealots are generally unyielding. They know little about the play of opinion and much about dying for their convictions. Abolitionists were no exception. Scores of them were convinced that to let women into their organizations was to raise an inflammable second issue which would ruin their own cause.

The camp to which Garrison and the Motts belonged was just as sure that the denial of free speech and action to women was identical with the evil which denied freedom to the Negro. This cleavage of viewpoint nearly wrecked the World Anti-Slavery Convention called at Freemason's Hall in London, in the spring of 1840.

FIVE FOR FREEDOM

To this convention went James and Lucretia Mott as delegates, carrying credentials from the Pennsylvania Society. Many men and a handful of other women delegates from American antislavery organizations accompanied them.

FIVE

Landing at Liverpool, they had time before the convention for a leisurely journey by coach to London, stopping at points of interest on the way. It cannot be said that either James or Lucretia were impressed by the splendor of historic castles or any other monuments to feudal tradition. They were too thoroughly Yankee. Rather scornfully, Lucretia dubbed them "catchpennies." Her eyes and ears were atuned to something quite different. She was far more interested in cotton mills and factories, never missing a detail which concerned the lives of laborers in a foreign land. She would have been blind indeed had she not noticed that there were a great many poor in England at this period—underpaid, overworked, and wretchedly housed.

A visit to the British Museum climaxed her boredom with sights. "I slept while the others looked," she admitted afterwards, without the slightest embarrassment.

Both she and James were shocked at the contrast between the wealth of the landed aristocracy and the poverty of the lower classes. Lucretia's reaction to parade and pomp could not be concealed in her diary. Of a specially arranged meeting with the Duchess of Sutherland, she made this single dry comment: "Much fuss when they arrived in a coach and four grays, with outriders and six servants in livery."

On the other hand she found Lady Byron worth knowing, because she was deeply interested in education and social betterment. The fact was that Lucretia held a small but select court in London, despite the warnings of orthodox American Quakers to their English brethren to have nothing to do with those dangerous "Hicksites," the Motts. Under her Quaker composure Lucretia was a firebrand who ignited people whether they agreed with her or not.

The dour Thomas Carlyle, always contentious, had to admire her ability to argue him down without heat. But Benjamin Haydon, painter of historical subjects, could not abide what he called her "infidel notions." He decided not to give her a front place in the picture he had been commissioned to paint of the convention.

This punishment Lucretia never noticed, being totally devoid of vanity. Nor did Haydon's small revenge alter the general opinion that she was "lioness" of the convention, even though she and the other women delegates were allowed no part in the proceedings.

For Lucretia and her companions were dismayed to learn, on their arrival in London, that British antislavery officials were not going to recognize the credentials of women delegates and had never anticipated their coming. Lucretia refused to accept so absurd a ruling. American antislavery societies had appointed men and women, choosing those best fitted for the mission regardless of sex. What right had a handful of Englishmen to reverse that decision?

At Mark Moore's, the lodging house in London where the American company had engaged rooms, there was constant collision over the question during the few days before the convention opened. Over dinner and tea to which they invited their English hosts, and at social functions to which they in turn were asked, the conflict went on with polite restraint but persistence.

Convention officials found the demure Mrs. Mott as immovable as Gibraltar. They tried tact and persuasion. It was a pity, wasn't it, to inject discord into so public an occasion? Why not yield a relatively unimportant point? Other women delegates would follow her leadership and the disagreement be forgotten.

But no, she insisted; who had given the Executive Committee authority to decide whether or not women delegates were acceptable? The question must be raised to the convention itself. There were never any ready answers to the points she made.

Meanwhile, those men delegates who supported the women were reserving their ammunition for the opening. Preliminary skirmishes therefore were all Lucretia's. She got in adroit thrusts on the subject with uncanny dexterity. It took wit and skill to fence lightly but with deadly aim, keeping within diplomatic bounds, so that no hurt was done to the cause of abolition.

All this sparring back and forth at Mark Moore's delighted young Elizabeth Cady Stanton, bride of a few weeks, who had come on her wedding journey to London with her delegate husband, Henry Stanton. A girl of brilliant intellect, she was fascinated most of all by the alert little Quaker lady whose repartee was so pat, whom the thunder of masculine authority and British officialdom neither scared nor subdued. At first she had been dismayed at the prospect of staying under the same roof with the redoubtable Mrs. Mott, of whom she had heard no good during her crossing from New York. For Elizabeth and Henry Stanton had sailed with James G. Birney, one of the most violent objectors to women in abolition circles. Arriving in London under his banner, she feared she would be both unpopular and defenseless among all those strong-minded lady delegates. But once at Mark Moore's, Elizabeth changed her mind. Mrs. Mott welcomed the shy young stranger with great kindness. Moreover the able and interesting women in her circle impressed Elizabeth deeply.

It did not take her long to see what had not been clear before; that a second form of enslavement, not so cruel as the Negro's but equally stultifying, had become an issue between these would-be emancipators. Elizabeth found herself wishing that her husband had not become involved with those who opposed Mrs. Mott—the side to which, she was quickly discovering, most of the bigots belonged.

Then one day at the crowded dinner table at Mark Moore's, someone talking with Lucretia Mott made an indefensible statement about women, and Elizabeth jumped impulsively into the fray with an indignant retort.

There was an instant's dead silence as the company took in the fact of a desertion in the Birney ranks and the arrival of a new champion to the women's lists. At the same time, Lucretia, sitting across the table, sent her young friend a look of searching appraisal.

It dawned on Elizabeth Cady Stanton then that she had started on a road from which there was no retreat, and that a pioneer traveler, rich in experience, had signaled a welcome. She seized the proffered friendship eagerly. There had been no one before to whom she could confide her secret rebellions, her heresies and doubts, her longing to try unexplored paths.

From now on, whenever she was alone with Lucretia Mott, the two became absorbed in talk.

As a result of Lucretia's stubborn pressure, women delegates were admitted to the convention hall, but only provided they sat behind a curtained enclosure where they could not be seen, and did not open their mouths. A gracious concession accepted with the irony it deserved.

Opening ceremonies began peacefully enough, out of respect for the venerable English abolitionist, Thomas Clarkson, who gave the first address. Immediately afterwards, however, Wendell Phillips, true to his promise, rose to force a vote on the recognition of women delegates. Self-assured and urbane, no one was better fitted to introduce a dangerous topic as though it contained no explosive. He proposed forming a committee to draw up "a correct list" of the members of this convention, with instructions to include in such list all persons bearing credentials from any antislavery body.

Hardly had he sat down before the opposition, mostly clergymen, jumped up with cries of "No, no!" Members of the so-called "New Organization" joined them.

The hubbub was temporarily quieted by the indignant speech of Dr. J. Bowring, a member of Parliament. "What," he thundered, "are American women coming to England as representatives ... not to be welcomed with honor? Not to be put in seats of dignity?" Quite obviously they were not, being already segregated behind a curtain like sheep in a pen.

All the clergymen, both English and American, were by now on their feet, thumping their Bibles with excitement. It was a defiance of Holy Writ, they cried, to permit women to speak in public. The limits of woman's sphere were clearly defined in the Bible. Timeworn allusions to Eve, her humble origin from a rib and her seduction by the serpent were repeated over and over with slight variations, until George Bradburn of Massachusetts rose from his seat, exasperation adding inches to his impressive bulk.

He would make a "bonfire of every Bible in the universe," he roared, if he believed it sanctioned "the slavery of women."

Before the clergy could recover from this blast, the floor was next seized by English Quakers, all afraid of James's and Lucretia's Hicksite influence in England and bent on foiling it. Against the Quakers, James then took up the fight in his patient but determined way, smarting from an attack from that quarter.

Meanwhile, in the corner in which they were herded from view, the "weaker sex" listened in derisive silence to the childish uproar of the strong. Lucretia held her peace, only too aware of the motives behind Quaker opposition. She was beginning to think there was more dignity in *not* joining a body of emancipators, so "swallowed up," as she put it, "in the littleness of putting woman down" that the purpose of their meeting seemed forgotten.

Arguments and recriminations flew back and forth the whole of that first day and ended in hopeless defeat for the women delegates. But one incident cheered Elizabeth Cady

Stanton. Her husband performed a right-about-face and put in an eloquent plea for the woman's side.

At the end of the day, Lucretia and Elizabeth, greatly stirred by the venom displayed and the nonsense voiced, decided to start a crusade for woman's rights as soon as possible after their return to America.

William L. Garrison, arriving late at the convention, learned that women had been refused a share in its deliberations and thereupon refused a share in them himself. To the dismay of officials he sat during the remainder of the convention in the spectators' gallery.

Critics called Garrison's act quixotic and futile, but it was no cavalier gesture for the most prominent figure in abolition ranks to refrain from a part in its world congress. His stand was taken at real cost to himself, and it gave woman's rights a place of importance no other masculine supporter had yet conceded it. Garrison never forgot that Lucretia had been the first to welcome him from a Baltimore jail. He paid that debt at the London convention.

Eight years, however, were to pass before Lucretia and Elizabeth Cady Stanton fulfilled the vow made to each other in London. On their return home, circumstances separated them. Elizabeth became a mother and her time was taken up with children.

Back in Philadelphia, after their one interlude of travel, James and Lucretia stepped into harness again. In the prolonged struggle for Negro emancipation during the next twenty years, their ardor for risks never cooled.

Lucretia cared nothing for appearances. She was quite capable of making a scene in public when she thought the occasion warranted it. Abolitionists had been warned not to be seen walking or talking with Negroes on the street or in public conveyances, a threat she scornfully ignored.

How much vilification of herself she read in the papers will never be known. The words "brazen infidel" were often attached to her name. Her preaching was frequently called "infernal," her acts "treason." Like many another public figure she developed an inner defense against both epithets and flattery.

But when the Civil War broke out and abolition became a popular Northern cause, many Quakers who had once violently opposed her now itched to be counted among her acquaintances. Amused and undeceived, she kept her reflections on that subject to herself. It was enough that her people's shameful indifference had come to an end.

Lucretia's heart and soul were in the slavery issue to the finish, but even so, she who had set fire to the issue of woman's rights found time to encourage and support the movement's feeble beginning. Always an inspiration and a guide to younger women, and to Elizabeth Cady Stanton in particular, she urged them into leadership and assumed what tasks she had strength for as the years advanced.

True to Nantucket traditions of open-handed hospitality and fireside discussion, no small part of her crusading had taken place under her own roof. Around her dinner table, over afternoon tea, at her lighted hearth, social questions were thrashed out, converts were made, fellow crusaders comforted and heartened for their next combat. Lucretia had become one of Philadelphia's eminent citizens. Her renown as a great hostess spread beyond these shores.

There were few notable visitors to America who did not seek an introduction to the Motts, Charles Dickens among them. Callers with great names, however, received no different welcome from the humblest. Robert Purvis and other educated Negroes were frequent dinner guests. To Englishmen this was no shock, but many an American of those days had to choose between his prejudices and the friendship of the Motts.

At length, Lucretia's lavish spending of herself to further enlightenment and freedom had to be curtailed. Even when she refused pleas to preside or to speak on public occasions, there was no rest from callers at home. She and James decided regretfully to sell the Philadelphia house in which they had spent so many hours of rare fellowship and fateful suspense. They moved to a small farmhouse eight miles from the city. Here more leisure was possible and thoughtful solitude was uninterrupted. It remained their home until the end.

Against the thrust and battle of Lucretia's life stands James, staunch supporter and tireless, devoted co-worker. No more loyal and self-effacing champion of freedom has existed in America than James Mott.

He was simple and honest and benignly tolerant. Children loved him. His brief advice to parents contains more wisdom than most volumes on the subject: "Never threaten and never promise reward, and be very careful to consider before you say 'No'; say 'Yes' as often as you can."

James died twelve years before Lucretia. Venerable soldier that she was by that time, she carried on with pathetic gallantry, finding small, humble ways to be useful at home when feebleness ended her public work.

Lucretia was beautiful in old age. Her outward form seemed a transparent shell, her clear, valiant spirit all but disembodied. She was eighty-seven before she drifted through peaceful sleep to the long rest she had earned.

Thousands gathered for the brief outdoor burial service, conducted as she would have wished it in tranquil, unbroken Quaker silence. As the crowd lingered reverently, loath to go without some last tribute, a muffled voice broke the stillness.

"Will no one say anything?"

"Who can speak," came the low answer. "The preacher is dead."

II

Elizabeth Cady Stanton

"Never forget that if I have done anything for the women of my country, it is not I—it is Susan and I."

Elizabeth Cady Stanton

"George Borrow, in his singular narrative, *The Romany Rye*, states that the sale of a wife, with a halter round her neck, is still a legal transaction in England. It must be done in the cattle market, as if she were a mare, 'all women being considered as mares by old English law, and indeed called mares in certain counties where old English is still preserved.'"

The History of Woman Suffrage (Vol. I)

"Many a wife is at present sold in the East End of London, as well as in Yorkshire, for a quart of beer or an ounce of thick twist."

London *Daily Mail*, March 1, 1899

ONE

Slow-rising fog clung to the treetops, obscuring the rolling hills of the Finger Lakes region, through which Elizabeth Cady Stanton drove. Each time the narrow country road dipped into a vale it sank also into a pocket of mist.

To Elizabeth, reining in her horses to a more cautious gait, the journey seemed to typify her own clouded thoughts. Since she and Henry had left Boston and come to live in Seneca Falls, mental depression had become almost a habit.

She had left home before the sun had burned off the morning mists, eager to make the most of this brief vacation from family cares. Lucretia Mott, whom she saw but rarely now, had written to say she was staying in nearby Waterloo with her Quaker friends, the Hunts. Would Elizabeth drive over?

She had needed no urging. What doors of the mind and spirit Lucretia had opened to her, on her unique wedding journey with Henry to the London Anti-Slavery Convention! Other experiences of the trip had faded to insignificance now.

"What impressed you most in Europe?" Elizabeth had been asked on her return to the States, and she remembered replying, without the slightest hesitation, "Lucretia Mott!"

In contrast to those memorable early years of her marriage, the present seemed barren indeed. She might just as well be living in a wilderness as on the outskirts of Seneca Falls, isolated from most of her interests and companions. At first she had thrown all her enthusiasm into fixing over the old house into which she and Henry had moved, but now the fun of reconstruction was over, her days were filled with humdrum tasks.

Because Henry had to be away on legal business much of the time, the management of three lively boys and a big household fell almost entirely on her own shoulders. Irish immigrants were her nearest neighbors. They were the only hired help to be found in this locality and added social responsibilities to her family cares.

Women of the squalid settlement in the valley soon learned that the brisk young mistress in whose kitchen they were reluctantly introduced to order and cleanliness, could be a stout ally when menfolk got drunk, and that when children fell ill her common sense was worth a doctor's prescription. However, this sort of life to Elizabeth was no substitute for the one she had enjoyed.

The house of her cousin Gerrit Smith, in Peterboro, New York, was a rallying point for liberal thinkers, writers, politicians. There she had met her husband, the well-known abolitionist speaker, Henry Stanton. She was used to holding her own in keen debate on books and public questions, and now, ever since her arrival in Seneca Falls, she had felt trapped in a domestic vacuum shared with children and servants. No wonder so many women had undeveloped minds and became an easy prey to their nerves.

If ever there was a skilled housewife and devoted mother, that one was Lucretia Mott, but her tart comments on domestic drudgery, the employment of women's hands to the neglect of their minds, was well known. Lucretia could speak with authority, since, in spite of the heavy household burdens which modest means and a large family had imposed on her, she had made the most of her great gifts.

Looking over the past, Elizabeth remembered that her own life in a small town near Albany had been affluent by comparison. She had grown up in a roomy, Victorian mansion surrounded by spacious grounds. There had been horses and a pony in her father's stables. She had never lacked for comforts or luxuries.

Judge Cady was Johnstown's most prominent lawyer, so Elizabeth and her four sisters had been given advantages beyond the reach of their classmates at Johnstown Academy. Elizabeth had even had all the education she wanted—for a brief while.

Possibly it was because she was the Judge's daughter that the Academy broke precedent to let her study Greek and higher mathematics with the boys. But it was her own hard work and determination which carried off the prize in Greek. In girlhood she tried hard to compensate her father for the death of an older brother, his only son; a naïve ambition which spurred her studies until the truth was forced upon her that a daughter's achievements evoked more embarrassment than pride from Judge Cady.

This humiliating discovery was a sequel to one made earlier, which had puzzled her in childhood. Her father's law offices were attached to the house, and Elizabeth noticed that the women who sought his advice left more often than not in tears. The little girl decided that women must have very special troubles, beyond even a judge's power to remedy.

"I cannot change the law," she heard her father remonstrate with a weeping client. And again, "The law, unfortunately, does not recognize a wife's claims, madam." Or, "Your husband's action is sustained by law; there is no way I can help you."

The law! It was always the law that was responsible, and Elizabeth knew where it was—on the pages of her father's big books. In answer to her own troubled questions he had shown her paragraph after incriminating paragraph. The solution seemed transparent to a child.

Why not cut those laws out with a pair of scissors, every one which was unfair to women? Fortunately for Judge Cady, she confided this scheme to Flora Campbell, an old client who had been impoverished by her husband, and whose difficulties, Elizabeth assured her, would vanish as soon as she could carry out her plan.

Forewarned by Mrs. Campbell, Judge Cady explained the situation more clearly, suggesting a remedy which to his great exasperation was to be remembered and later acted upon. "Suppose my whole library should burn," he reasoned with his small daughter, "that would not benefit women at all. But there is something you can do when you are grown. Go down to Albany and talk to the legislators. Tell them all you have seen in this office, the suffering of women robbed of their inheritance and left dependent on worthless sons. If you can persuade them to pass new laws, the old ones will be a dead letter."

As she grew older, her father's students who were intimates

of the family discovered her childish obsession and teased her unmercifully with their newly acquired knowledge of marital law.

"If in due time you should be my wife," remarked Henry Bayard, when she showed him her Christmas gift of a necklace and bracelet, "those ornaments would be mine. I could take them and lock them up, and you could never wear them except with my permission. I could even exchange them for a cigar, and you could watch them evaporate in smoke." He blew an imaginary ring as he spoke, noting with amusement that Elizabeth's hand closed unconsciously on the beads at her throat.

"I haven't the slightest intention of earning my living," another boy would add, "since I intend to marry a woman of property."

"Earn your own money, and keep it from your husband?" a third countered her indignant retort. "You can't. A wife's earnings are not legally her own; they are her husband's."

The more she sputtered the more they baited her. Wife-beating was an even more amusing subject. The only legal restriction on a husband was the size of the stick he used, they informed her.

"No *gentleman* takes advantage of these laws—naturally," and the condescension of this assurance always brought her temper to the boiling point.

At seventeen she had been incredibly naïve and defenseless, but after her meeting with Lucretia Mott she had never been so guileless again. How nimbly in London, and with what shrewdness and urbanity had Lucretia parried the antifeminist attacks of the convention officials and the clergy who refused to recognize the women delegates. Each one of her polite an-

swers had carried a small sting. Elizabeth's whip flicked a road-
side weed in amused retrospect.

In girlhood it had never dawned on her until her final year
at school that she could not go on to college with the boys in
her class. When she learned with shock that colleges closed
their doors to women, she was stirred afresh.

Resentfully she tried a pallid substitute. Troy Seminary,
Emma Willard's daring new experiment in female education,
offered mild courses in literature, mathematics and philosophy,
besides the usual training in social deportment and the domestic arts. It was better than staying at home.

At Troy, Elizabeth learned enough about the segregation
of the sexes to make her a confirmed believer in coeducation.
The first time she heard someone in her dormitory call, "Heads
out!" she rushed to the window with the rest, expecting to
see a circus go by.

"Boys! Don't you see them? Over there!" the girls squealed
an explanation, when she looked her bewilderment.

"Is that all? I've seen boys all my life," and Elizabeth turned
impatiently away.

For all the absurdities of life at the Seminary, Emma Willard, its founder, did have extremely advanced ideas for her
period. She later introduced physiology to girls, thereby
scandalizing the town of Troy. Shocked mothers who visited
the first class felt their modesty affronted; several of the girls
fainted; and, at the insistence of parents, paper had to be
pasted over the diagrams in the textbooks to spare the sensi-
bilities of their daughters.

Unfortunately, Mrs. Willard's views on religious revivals
were not at all advanced. During a period of six weeks, Semi-

nary students were treated to lurid descriptions of hell-fire and other features of the nether regions in store for unbelievers.

Hosts of superstitious fears were now added to those already fixed in childhood in Elizabeth's fertile imagination by an old Scottish Calvinist nurse. Her terror caused sleepless nights and affected her health. Home again, among rational people who reasoned her dread away, she quite naturally avoided doctrinal religion after that as a nightmare.

Nor had the ranting of the clergy at the World Anti-Slavery Convention in London lured her back to the fold. Almost she could have become a Quaker under Lucretia's sweet and liberal influence, except for the sorry exhibition put on by the English Friends at the same time.

Elizabeth halted her horses at the top of a long, steep hill. Beyond and below her lay Waterloo, where the solid green of trees was broken by rooftops. The glint of a church spire turned her thoughts to religion again. All that claptrap about woman being the inferior sex needed to be corrected with logic. So long as woman's subjection was preached from the pulpits, there'd be little chance for advance. Victim in youth herself of false theological teachings, she would like nothing better than to help wipe them out.

But uprooting old beliefs was not as quick nor as easy as it sounded, Elizabeth had to admit ruefully. A good illustration was her father's clutch on conservative views and customs. How strongly he had objected to her marrying Henry Stanton and, worse still, how nearly she had yielded to his will.

In Judge Cady's opinion—and a judge was used to having his opinions respected—abolitionists were fanatics and visionaries incapable of earning a living. His daughter, he predicted, would be dragged through public disgrace, to say nothing of poverty. Only when she had been compelled to make up her mind quickly, almost on the eve of Henry's departure for the London Anti-Slavery Convention, had she found the courage to marry him.

Suppose she had not chosen a liberal thinker? A man who welcomed the same qualities of independence in his wife? Suppose she had married one of those strutting students of her father's, who knew a great deal too much about a husband's legal privileges! Elizabeth shivered. She had very narrowly escaped the fate of an amiable domestic slave, or, more likely, a soured one. She knew plenty of both types.

For the moment she was most certainly tied hand and foot to the kitchen and nursery, but at least it was none of Henry's wishing. It was due to his health that they had been forced to leave Boston and move inland to hill country. In the Seneca Falls region, moreover, Henry's business prospects were excellent, a sufficient reason for remaining there and confounding her father with the spectacle of an abolitionist who was also a successful lawyer!

TWO

Elizabeth had driven half through Waterloo by this time and found the street she sought. On the verandah of the house she was approaching sat a group of women in Quaker garb. Yes—the smallest with the organdy cap—she was Lucretia Mott, without a doubt. Elizabeth turned her horses into the drive.

"Oh, but we hoped thee would arrive early," Lucretia answered her apologies as her team was led away. "There is so much to tell since we met last in Boston. This is Jane Hunt, our hostess, Mary McClintock and my sister Martha Wright. But thee hardly needs an introduction. I have been telling them what a champion thee was of the woman's side at the London Anti-Slavery Convention."

The three who greeted Elizabeth for the first time saw a young matron barely thirty, of average height, on the edge of plumpness. A wide-brimmed straw bonnet framed round, blooming cheeks and brown hair, hanging Victorian fashion, in ringlets. Good humor glowed in her face and through her laughter, but all during the flow of exuberant talk, her keen blue glance took in Lucretia's friends, measured them and liked them. She always warmed to the task of making new friends, finding a new audience. She was a born actress, unconsciously creating a drama out of the most inconsequential things.

"You can see for yourselves," she appealed to her listeners now with outspread hands, after a long, humorous account of her life in Seneca Falls, "I'm about to die of an intellectual repression!"

It was always to be one of her favorite complaints, that of repression. As time went on and she was deluged with public as well as family obligations, her energy and spirit seemed unquenchable. Watching her buoyancy now, her audience of four could not help smiling.

But out of Elizabeth's banter there soon emerged a serious object. As far as she was concerned, the time had never been more ripe to start a woman's movement, the one she and Lucretia had dreamed of eight years ago. What better place than Seneca Falls to launch it? Did her friends realize that New York State had recently passed a bill protecting the property rights of married women?

No high motives had prompted the bill, to be sure. It had been sponsored by wealthy Dutch farmers of the Hudson Valley region, as tightfisted and hardheaded a group as existed. They were tired of seeing the farms they had given their daughters for dowry pass into the hands of their wastrel sons-in-law.

Just the same it was the best possible moment to publicize other injustices to women. By afternoon, Elizabeth had worked her companions to a pitch of enthusiasm where they were ready to call a convention. Together they drafted the following notice for insertion next day in the Seneca Falls *Courier*:

WOMAN'S RIGHTS CONVENTION
"A convention to discuss the social, civil and religious condition and rights of women will be held in the Wesleyan Chapel at Seneca Falls, N.Y., on Wednesday and Thursday, the 19th and 20th of July current; commencing at 10 o'clock A. M."

The opening day, the notice went on to read, was for women only. The second day all were welcome to hear Lucretia Mott of Philadelphia and other ladies and gentlemen address the convention.

No sooner drafted than handed to the postman as he made his rounds, after which the five bold pioneers sat back and looked at each other, slightly aghast. They had but four days to prepare the program they had glibly announced. Moreover, Elizabeth, the most fertile in ideas, had to go home in two days. How did one go about organizing a movement? That night they confessed themselves stalled, but not yet driven to seek masculine advice.

Next morning, however, as they struggled hour after hour to formulate a constitution and a set of resolutions, Elizabeth realized that the task was too big for novices. They began leafing through reports of antislavery organizations and temperance societies, but none of them embodied anything like their own passionately felt convictions.

"Oh, for a Jefferson!" thought Elizabeth.

The idea was so persistent that finally she got out the

Declaration of Independence. Reading its stirring phrases aloud to the others, as they sat around the paper-littered mahogany table in Mary McClintock's parlor, they all saw how aptly and with what few changes it could be turned into a "Woman's Declaration of Sentiments."

> "When in the course of human events, it becomes necessary for one portion of the family of man to assume among the people of the earth a position different from that which they have hitherto occupied, but one to which the laws of nature and of nature's God entitle them, a decent respect to the opinions of mankind requires that they should declare the causes that impel them to such a course.
>
> "We hold these truths to be self-evident: that all men and women are created equal...."

The writing went swiftly now as they paraphrased line after line of the grand old document.

> "The history of mankind is a history of repeated injuries and usurpations on the part of man toward woman, having in direct object the establishment of an absolute tyranny over her. To prove this let facts be submitted to a candid world."

Following this sentence in the original Declaration, the Colonists had listed eighteen injustices imposed on them by the British king.

"Why not complete the parallel with eighteen wrongs of

our own?" suggested Elizabeth. "They won't be hard to think up."

Actual laws were important to cite, and since these needed checking, they appealed to a friendly Waterloo attorney for loan of his statute books.

"Your grievances must be grievances indeed, when you are obliged to go to books to find them out," he twitted as they marched off with them, but they were so well rewarded by what they found that his jibe fell flat.

First on their list they placed the charge which was to launch a campaign of seventy-two years' duration:

"He (man) has never permitted her (woman) to exercise her inalienable right to the elective franchise."

"He has made her, if married, in the eye of the law, civilly dead," read the fifth grievance. How well Elizabeth remembered that taunt of her father's students, because of its gruesome implications.

And the sixth: "He has taken from her all right in property, even to the wages she earns."

"He has made her an irresponsible being, as she can commit many crimes with impunity, provided they can be done in the presence of her husband..." This seventh was the fruit of considerable research and quite a plum!

Divorce laws, denying women freedom from dissolute partners and robbing them of their children, were also listed.

Elizabeth leaned back in her chair, satisfied that her early training as an attorney's daughter was not wasted. She could, after all, thank certain half-baked young men for their share in her legal education.

"How about the *unwritten* laws now," she suggested,

"those which bar women from the best paid positions, from all the professions, except schoolteaching, from college degrees?"

"And from pulpits," finished Lucretia, the Quaker preacher.

That attended to, they wound up their Declaration with a list of unfair social codes and practices—chief in importance those which ostracized women for moral delinquency tolerated in men.

There remained now only a set of Resolutions which would determine the movement's purposes, to be presented and adopted by the convention. It was the ninth resolution, offered by Elizabeth, which, when it was first broached in Mary McClintock's parlor, caused consternation:

"*Resolved,*" it read, "that it is the duty of the women of this country to secure for themselves their sacred right to the elective franchise."

To understand why Elizabeth's resolution was so startling, one must remember that for a century the injustice of not being allowed to vote had been protested from time to time, but no one had yet suggested that women set out to win the ballot on their own initiative.

Moreover, the other resolutions merely repeated what the Declaration had already said, in somewhat different terms. Only Elizabeth's was a call for action.

Her four Quaker friends stared at their young collaborator in dismay.

"Why, Lizzie," cried Lucretia, "thee will make us ridiculous!"

Amazed in her turn, Elizabeth turned red with mortification and hurt. Was Lucretia, who had faced angry mobs without flinching, suddenly beginning to quail before public opinion?

Could she not see that until women had an equal voice in government, they were powerless to safeguard their "rights"? "Thee moves too fast," she heard Lucretia add. "We must go slowly."

Had there been time to talk the difference out, Lucretia might have argued that in the slavery issue, right or wrong, justice and injustice were clearly defined, while the woman's cause would be opposed by tradition, sentiment, custom, smug conventions and entrenched theological beliefs. Against the self-righteous pedantry of the Quaker sect, she had battled unsuccessfully a great part of her life. She knew no more stubborn enemy to progress.

Almost certainly, Elizabeth would have disagreed. Prudence was foreign to her, half-measures impossible. And she was too independent to yield her convictions, even for Lucretia whom she revered. Perhaps it was just as well. It was the drive of her unreckoning youth which headed the movement for Woman's Rights toward a definite goal.

She said little in reply now, for she was on the point of leaving, and all the arrangements for the convention at Seneca Falls had been left to her. Hurrying home, she decided, on the way, to show Henry her resolution, confident as she was that he would support it.

But Henry amazed her. He argued so emphatically against it in fact, that Elizabeth began to bristle resentfully. Hold a woman's rights convention by all means, said he, especially since Mrs. Mott would be sponsoring it, but Elizabeth would certainly turn the meeting into a fiasco if she demanded the franchise. Had she no realization of the ridicule her idea would encounter? Very well—if she insisted on making a laughing

stock of herself, and of him too—he, Henry, would stay away
from the convention!

It was their first heated disagreement, and the more conjugal
advice Henry gave the more obstinate Elizabeth became. However, there was one person whose unprejudiced judgment she
could be sure of and whose counsel she would seek. If he
brought valid objections—but then, she was sure he would
see eye to eye with her.

This person was Frederick Douglass, the tall, handsome
Negro abolitionist, who, though a fugitive slave, had the
dignity and bearing of a king. She had met Douglass in Boston
abolition circles and found him an ardent sympathizer with
women's wrongs. He had been invited to speak at the Seneca
Falls convention. Lucretia's presence would draw him, she
knew, if nothing else did. Elizabeth resolved to have a word
with him before the meeting.

In the meantime, having alienated Henry from her project,
she found sticking to her convictions a solitary and chilling
occupation. She had moments of sheer panic as the day of the
convention neared. From the beginning, Lucretia had made
it clear that while she would lend her advice and support,
others less involved than she in abolition work must bear the
brunt of the new movement. And so when a note from Lucretia arrived regretting that she might have to be absent from
the convention on account of James's sudden illness, Elizabeth
had an instant's temptation to call the whole thing off.

But her preparations had gone too far. All she could do
now was to make doubly sure that her own speech was
adequate. She wrote it in feverish snatches, between the hundred household emergencies that arose daily: the pudding Mag-

gie scorched; the overturned pan of milk; Neil's thumb, cut by the axe he had been forbidden to touch; the stone young Henry threw into the library window, and the squabble that resulted in Gerrit's bloody nose. The three would not have been hers had they not been full of mischief and enterprise.

By dint of shouting down her misgivings, when she was not shouting at the boys, she managed to feel ready for anything when the sun rose on the fateful July 19. And suddenly like a change in tide, things began to flow her way.

THREE

Well before the hour set, as she and Neil were airing the little church for the expected guests, James Mott, looking as benignly placid as ever, if a trifle seedy, disentangled himself from rugs and lunchbaskets and thrust his long legs out of the buggy in which he and his wife had driven over from Waterloo. After him stepped Lucretia and Martha Wright. Elizabeth breathed a thankful sigh. No convention could be a total loss with the Motts present.

Soon Frederick Douglass arrived, his magnificent black-bearded head conspicuous above the rest.

"Tell me," she asked, drawing him aside, "what do you consider the one most important privilege for the Negro to gain, the key which will open the door to all his other freedoms?"

"The vote," answered Douglass without hesitation.

"Good," exclaimed Elizabeth triumphantly, "then surely you approve the same principle for women? Will you speak for this, if I read it?" and she handed him her resolution.

But even with Douglass's promise of support, Elizabeth felt a stab of apprehension when carriages began to disgorge more people than she had dared expect. *She* had initiated this gathering, which could either be remembered historically or degenerate into a farce, as Henry predicted. Would she or would she not offer her resolution? Lucretia, meantime, was serenely unaware that her disapproval had not settled the matter. As she greeted people and attended to last-minute details, Elizabeth underwent agonies of vacillation.

In spite of the fact that the first day of the convention had been advertised as open to women only, a number of men besides Douglass and James Mott put in an appearance. Surprised and gratified, the sponsors, Lucretia, Elizabeth, Martha Wright and Mary McClintock, hastily decided to admit them all. The four of them were still humiliatingly unfamiliar with parliamentary procedure. James was just the chairman they needed.

Elizabeth felt her qualms subside as he called the convention to order, and Lucretia, used to thinking on her feet, developed her opening remarks with clarity and order. She sketched broadly the many handicaps under which women labored, and explained the necessity for them to band together as a class in order to better their condition. Lucretia was the only woman present capable of speaking extemporaneously.

Her sister, Martha, had published a few short satirical articles on woman's sphere. These furnished a note of humor. Mary McClintock read an excellent paper of her own, after which it was Elizabeth's turn. She, too, read her maiden speech, and with a coolness that was encouraging, considering her dry throat.

Two of the men brought material of lively interest. One of them told how he had personally helped the passage in Albany of the property rights bill for married women. The other had court records showing how easily, under existing laws, a husband could gain control of his wife's money and property.

The meeting closed in a burst of animated discussion. Elizabeth reported triumphantly back to Henry that no discordant incident had marred the first day of the convention. It was too soon though to crow very loudly, she realized. Tomorrow the assembly would either adopt or reject the Declaration of Sentiments, and decide the fate of all the resolutions, her own included.

A short, auburn-haired woman, not as reluctant to be seen and heard as most of her timorous sisters, had already announced positively that, although she agreed with the proposals of the convention, she could not approve those sections of the Declaration which encouraged women to step outside their purely domestic role. She was especially shocked by the disrespect of the ladies present for the opinions of the clergy. Such policies, if persisted in, would certainly ruin their cause, she warned, and having said her say firmly, wrapped herself in disdainful silence.

Elizabeth recognized her as a leader in Seneca Falls temperance circles, a lady whose influence could not be lightly discounted. Her name was Amelia Bloomer. Mrs. Bloomer's talk was pious and prudent, and the hint of superiority in her manner rankled. Elizabeth went home, chagrined that the one woman in Seneca Falls from whom she might have expected support had no genuine crusading spirit.

In the little Wesleyan Church next day, the convention reassembled to define the new movement and outline its purposes. The Declaration of Sentiments was quickly adopted, with a few minor changes. Sixty-eight women and thirty-two men signed it, but not Mrs. Bloomer. She, having predicted its certain ridicule, "stood aloof and laughed," much to Elizabeth's annoyance.

However, Amelia Bloomer was more honest than those who cravenly withdrew their signatures from the Declaration as soon as her prophecy came true. She, at least, was a frank conformist, whose caution was wasted in the end, since her name is now chiefly remembered for a rash experiment in dress which she never initiated.

The Declaration once signed, Elizabeth waited tensely to present her resolution. Hesitation swung her first one way, then another. If she kept silence, she would despise herself afterwards for a coward; if she spoke, thunders of disapproval would resound. Through her confusion Mary McClintock's voice penetrated, reading the eighth resolution:

"*Resolved*, that woman has too long rested satisfied in the circumscribed limits which corrupt customs and a perverted application of the Scriptures have marked out for her, and that it is time she should move in the enlarged sphere which her great Creator has assigned her."

"I'm not asking any more than that," Elizabeth reasoned silently, "simply that women fulfill their destiny." And with that she banished indecision for good.

Meanwhile—"The ayes have it!" announced James, as Mary's resolution passed over Mrs. Bloomer's manifest disapproval. His hammer struck the table a final rap.

Elizabeth rose quickly, the import of what she was about to do lifting her suddenly out of that small, closely packed church into her niche in history. Her voice, cutting the silence, seemed not her own, but the voice of a new order. She spoke slowly and distinctly.

"*Resolved,* that it is the duty of the women of this country to secure to themselves their sacred right to the elective franchise."

Amid a hush of amazement, she sat down.

Despite Lucretia, in defiance of Henry, she had planted her flag on the ramparts. She would keep it flying, however furiously the storm broke.

A gasp of astonishment heralded the storm's approach. Turning, Elizabeth met Lucretia's accusing look with one of bland innocence, her eyebrows raised impishly. Lucretia, who loved audacity no matter how ill-timed, felt amusement pierce her exasperation. Before her quick wit could redeem the situation, however, Frederick Douglass was on his feet eloquently supporting the resolution.

There followed a long, heated debate, at the end of which Elizabeth's motion was carried by a narrow margin. That it was passed over Lucretia's dissent was remarkable, considering the older woman's prestige. The sheer weight of its justice tipped the scales.

FOUR

Elizabeth had little heart for elation now she had won. There was sober truth in Lucretia's parting comment, that time alone would prove who was right, and time speedily produced all that Mrs. Bloomer had foreseen. The little upstate town, where a dangerously liberal idea had been born, became the immediate target for clergy and press.

Letters of retraction arrived immediately also, asking that their owners' signatures be stricken from the Declaration of Sentiments. There was no denying that Elizabeth's resolution and not the convention drew most of the fire, but Elizabeth, having sown the wind and reaped a tornado, found unexpected humor in her position. Some newspapers railed against the unwomanly conduct of females who called conventions, offered resolutions and made speeches, at "the expense of their more appropriate duties." Others sought to shame the "Amazons" by panegyrics on feminine charm.

With evident relish Lucretia sent Elizabeth a clipping from her home paper, the Philadelphia *Ledger*, which seemed to have forgotten the existence of its own fighting Quakeress.

"Our Philadelphia ladies not only possess beauty," chanted the *Ledger*, "but they are celebrated for discretion, modesty, and unfeigned diffidence, as well as wit, vivacity and good nature. Whoever heard of a Philadelphia lady setting up for a reformer, or standing out for women's rights? . . . Our ladies glow with a higher ambition. They soar to rule the hearts of their worshipers, and secure obedience by the sceptre of affection."

Meantime the instigators of the woman's revolution, undeterred by withering publicity, went on with their plan to reconvene in Rochester, New York, two weeks later. This second convention was almost unnoticed by the press. The idea of votes for women was still fantastic; it was to be caricatured, reviled and resisted for generations to come, but the shock of its first impact was spent.

Held in Rochester's Unitarian Church, this second convention was presided over entirely by women, contrary to both Lucretia's and Elizabeth's better judgment, who thought women still too untrained to attempt so prominent a role.

The experiment was admittedly rash. As no true "lady" of that era had ever raised her voice above a genteel murmur, hardly a speaker was heard beyond the first three rows. Impatient cries of "Louder! Louder!" punctuated the speeches, even though Abigail Bush, the chairman, had opened the convention with a plea for patience.

"Friends," she implored, her stiff crinoline petticoats hiding the quaking of her own knees, "we present ourselves here before you as an oppressed class, with trembling frames and faltering tongues, and we do not expect to be able to speak so as to be heard by all at first..."

Despite quaint apologies and behavior, this gathering, held in the auditorium of a big church and conducted by women, marked a real advance in their status; for in her own city of Philadelphia, Lucretia informed the assembly, a ladies' reform society had recently been told to meet in the church cellar and had been required to let men officiate.

Moreover, to the Rochester convention came two unobtrusive Quaker women, who listened attentively and left unnoticed. They were the mother and sister of Susan B. Anthony. It was their enthusiasm which first brought the woman's crusade to Susan's attention, although several more years were to elapse before her fateful meeting with Elizabeth.

In the interim, Elizabeth became the most colorful figure in the small and struggling movement. Gone were the days when she had been submerged in domestic boredom. Family cares and responsibilities had increased with the birth of a fourth child, Theodore, but with what a difference!

The Seneca Falls Convention had released in Elizabeth intellectual capacities which were to unfold more and more to the end of her life. No one else among that group of early women pioneers had her mastery of English and familiarity with law, or could parry the constant attacks from clergy and press with equal adroitness and wit.

Henry, now that he was used to the idea, raised no more objections to the franchise, and that was perhaps as far as a husband's enthusiasm could be expected to go. He felt, besides, no need to egg Elizabeth on. Quite the contrary. Seneca Falls was periodically rocked by her experiments, which is to say, periodically amused and stimulated. The "Conversation Club," which she organized to prod housewives out of an abysmal ignorance of public affairs, opened up "spheres" hitherto forbidden their sex.

Amelia Bloomer—enterprising, shrewd, and smarter than most—must have been cordially invited to join, for she and Elizabeth soon buried the hatchet and began to collaborate. Their common interest was in Mrs. Bloomer's periodical, *The Lily*—which, to her credit, was one of the first papers in this country to be owned, edited and printed singlehanded by a woman. *The Lily*, as its title implied, was dedicated to purity and temperance. As soon as Elizabeth became a contributor it was also dedicated to woman's advance.

FIVE

Meanwhile, back in Johnstown, Judge Cady, recovering from the shock of the Seneca Falls Convention and the diatribe which followed it, consoled himself with the thought that nothing short of public odium would teach his daughter a lesson. Now that Elizabeth's wild schemes had received a jolt, the family could settle back into comfortable obscurity. He even decided it was safe to risk a visit to Seneca Falls.

Arrived there however, he was chagrined to find Elizabeth not only undaunted, but preparing to give a speech on woman's rights in a nearby town. The situation, he felt, called for extreme measures, so he applied the parental curb which rarely fails.

"Are you getting ready, my dear, to lecture before a lyceum?" he demanded sternly one evening when they were alone.

"Yes, sir," came the defiant answer.

"Be sure then," and Judge Cady's brow clouded with the Jovian wrath that sat so well on Victorian fathers, "if you do so within my lifetime, it will be a very expensive lecture."

To this threat of disinheritance Elizabeth retorted with

more impudence than truth in view of the paltry ten dollars which was to be her lecture fee, "On the contrary—I intend it to be a very profitable one." Whereupon, picking up her candle, she marched off to bed through one door, while the Judge, decidedly shorn of his dignity, stalked out the other.

A little later, Elizabeth received a visit from her closest childhood playmate and cousin, Elizabeth Smith Miller, daughter of Cousin Gerrit Smith of Peterboro.

Gerrit Smith, an extreme liberal for his day, was branded by Judge Cady as an eccentric, and "Liz" was cut from the same piece of cloth as her father.

She arrived on Elizabeth's doorstep clad in pants, of a design never imagined before or since. True to family traditions, Liz faced the astounded gaze of Seneca Falls with a calm disregard for its opinion.

It was indelicate in those days for a woman to possess "legs." The word itself was banned from polite usage, and Mrs. Miller, though she defied fashion, was not deaf to the dictates of modesty.

Her trousers of black broadcloth covered her limbs, to be sure, but since they shamelessly proclaimed her a biped, Liz partly hid them under a full skirt, falling six inches below her knees. The total effect could hardly be called graceful. Over all this she wore a short, knee-length cape, when she went out, which left her trousers exposed and added yards to her girth. A wide-brimmed beaver hat, modishly trimmed with ostrich plumes and tied under her chin with a big bow, added the last bizarre touch.

As Elizabeth embraced her cousin, exclaiming over her original appearance, her eyes must have gleamed wickedly at the prospect of Henry's homecoming. He had ,surrendered with good grace, though a trifle late, on the question of the franchise. But her own heresies were going to seem pale beside this revolution in dress, launched under his roof.

Henry, however, had turned philosopher. Perhaps the Seneca Falls Convention had taught him the futility of arguing with a wife whose mind is made up. Then, too, his political duties (for he was now a State Senator) required his prolonged, and at such times convenient, absence in Albany. His reaction to Elizabeth's unconventional sprees was generally amused, often skeptical, and certainly more tolerant than that of her own family.

A husband's protest would have been ignored anyway, in view of the freedom Liz proceeded to demonstrate. She ran up and down stairs in the Stanton home without stopping to gather up her skirts. Neither corsets nor cumbersome petticoats made life a burden, so that household chores were accomplished in half the time. Outdoors, no trailing hems got soaked in the wet grass or soiled in mud and dust. Her "limbs" were unswathed and her step buoyant.

Inside of twenty-four hours, Elizabeth was won over to the new style. It was practical, healthful and liberating! With her usual impetuosity she ignored all obstacles until she met them head on. Aided and abetted by Liz, the two of them ripped yards and yards of superfluous material from her own gowns, refashioned them—and the crusade for sensible dress was on.

Their first sortie in their astonishing costumes was for the purpose of enlisting Mrs. Bloomer's enthusiasm and support. Those whose paths crossed theirs in the quiet streets of

Seneca Falls that day were struck dumb at the sight. The ribald jokes, the stares, nudges and guffaws came later, when the public believed what it saw.

Amelia Bloomer, strange to say, agreed to publicize the dress in her paper, *The Lily*, and for one of her conservative policies, this is difficult to explain. One can only hazard the guess that her estimate of Elizabeth and her madcap ideas had undergone a subtle change. Mrs. Bloomer was the wife of the village postmaster. Elizabeth had eminent friends and connections, whose names, dropped with unconscious frequency in her talk, could not have failed to carry weight.

Almost immediately, though, Mrs. Bloomer found herself confronted by two unwelcome choices. Having publicly sung the advantages of "the freedom dress," she must either brave the notoriety by donning it herself, or not wear it and be dubbed inconsistent. She chose the first alternative and reaped an unexpected reward.

Hundreds of letters soon swamped the little post office in Seneca Falls, asking for information about the dress and demanding a pattern. In no time the modest circulation of *The Lily* jumped to several thousand, and Mrs. Bloomer woke one delirious morning to find herself a celebrity. The costume Liz Miller had invented had become the "Bloomer dress," the sensation of the hour and focus of attention in the nation's press.

Mrs. Bloomer's own words hint a pleasurable excitement:

> "At the outset"—she wrote—"I had no idea of fully adopting the style, no thought of setting a fashion; no thought that my action would create an excitement through the civilized world, and give to

the style my name and the credit due Mrs. Miller. "I had gotten myself"—she added, not too ruefully—"into a position from which I could not recede, if I had desired to do so." Of the dress she insisted: "I was pleased with it and had no desire to lay it aside and would not let the ridicule of the press move me."

But Elizabeth, the real crusader, boasted no such thick skin. To begin with, "the shorts," as the dress was soon nicknamed, immediately affected Henry's political prospects adversely, causing his young wife both anxiety and remorse. It was the time for re-election of State Senators, and many a loyal Democrat who would ordinarily have voted for him, refused to support a candidate whose wife wore "the Bloomers."

"The severest trial of my life, dear Lizzie, I have just passed through," she confided to her cousin after the campaign was over and Henry safely elected. "My name was hawked about the streets and in all public meetings. Two men had a fight in one meeting about my hat. My dress," Elizabeth wound up her tale of martyrdom with a flourish of rhetoric, "was a subject of the severest animadversions."

It took real heroism to walk the streets unperturbed while village hooligans shouted "Breeches!" and chanted:

> *Heigh! Ho! The carrion crow,*
> *Mrs. Stanton's all the go;*
> *Twenty tailors take the stitches,*
> *Mrs. Stanton wears the breeches.*

"Had I counted the cost of the short dress, I would never have put it on," wailed poor Elizabeth. "However, I'll never take it off," she added defiantly, "for now it involves a principle of freedom."

She did take it off nevertheless, two years later, when the public had become more accustomed to it and her own family's sarcasm had subsided. Her father, with whom she was but recently reconciled, warned her angrily not to disgrace him in Johnstown with it, and her sisters in New York City, mortally afraid she would make a spectacle of herself there, were equally caustic.

Under pressure of criticism the dress was modified. Elizabeth experimented and improved it. Farm women designed their own version, finding it gave them a much-needed freedom, and doctors, who attributed many of the ills of their women patients to tight lacing and other dress restrictions, advocated its use in sanitariums.

It paved the way for later freedoms. Without it, who would have dared dream up the jaunty bicycle costume of the Gibson Girl period, or the gymnasium bloomer? Elizabeth Cady Stanton, Lucy Stone, and Susan B. Anthony, the three outstanding leaders, suffered greater martyrdom for the Bloomer dress than for any other phase of their crusade. One after another, as they became convinced the dress did more harm than good to the Cause, they gladly took it off. Only Mrs. Bloomer gave it up reluctantly, partly because both her name and her fame were identified with it and her slight figure looked better in it than most, and partly because her work for woman's rights, being less important than that of the others, did not subject her to the same searching glare of publicity.

The hooting and booing in the streets of Seneca Falls, following the debut of the Bloomer dress, had been directed at Elizabeth Cady Stanton because of her husband's prominent part in the elections. In the midst of public ridicule and the acid comments of her family, the guileless approval of her young sons was refreshing.

Neil, away at school, was old enough to be so embarrassed at the prospect of his mother's visiting him in a Bloomer dress, that he wrote an anguished letter to that effect. But in the innocent opinion of the other three, it made little difference what their high-spirited mother wore. She was their favorite companion, full of adventure herself and sympathetic to escapades.

It was not a family trait to be mere onlookers to any excitement, and so the Stanton children plunged early into the game of politics surging round them. Visitors to the house underwent sharp young scrutiny as to their party affiliations. Democrats were on the right side, Republicans the wrong. The whole Stanton family was on the right side with the exception of Theodore, still an infant, unable to declare his political faith. Theodore gave his brothers grave anxiety.

"Is the baby a Democrat?" Gerrit finally asked his mother, and received her laughing assurance.

SIX

Not many months after the start of the dress reform, the meeting which was to mean so much to the future advancement of women occurred. At this time, William Lloyd Garrison and George Thompson, the English abolitionist, were scheduled to speak in Seneca Falls, and Susan B. Anthony, then a young Rochester schoolteacher who had met Amelia Bloomer in temperance circles, accepted her invitation to attend the meeting. As the speakers were to be guests of Mrs. Stanton who was a friend of Mrs. Bloomer, the visit offered interest in more ways than one to Susan. She had heard much of Mrs. Stanton from her mother and sister who had gone to the Rochester Convention. Because Susan Anthony was a Quaker, she had never been humiliated by sex inequalities, and saw no special reason for a Woman's Movement.

However, she was curious to meet its most fearless champion.

No sooner had she arrived in Seneca Falls than Susan and Amelia Bloomer encountered Mrs. Stanton on the street. Amelia and Elizabeth were in their trouser dresses, to which the townsfolk gave only a derisive glance these days. By contrast, Susan probably never looked to better advantage in her graceful Quaker dress of soft gray delaine.

It could never have entered Mrs. Bloomer's head as she introduced the shy young teacher to Mrs. Stanton that the moment was historic and that a hidden affinity existed between these two quite opposite people.

Elizabeth belonged quite obviously to the fashionable world, even in her Bloomer pants. Their fine broadcloth and her richly furred cape spoke of an ample purse and a lavish personality. She greeted Susan with more than her usual impulsiveness and warmth, drawn to the silent Quaker girl by some inner strength she divined in her.

But Susan's hopes of being invited to the Stanton house were dashed almost immediately. As soon as she could, Elizabeth politely excused herself, leaving Amelia Bloomer and her guest standing there, blank and chagrined.

Elizabeth hurried home to her kitchen and her unskilled help. She was feasting the two lions of the abolition meeting, and had visions of a scorched roast and watery pudding. In addition, her four boys were capable of the most outrageous pranks in her brief absences from home.

Had they not recently floated Theodore, the baby, down the Seneca River in a homemade life preserver of small corks, and, at another time, perched him on a chimney pot on the roof, where he was discovered by a horrified passer-by? Rewarding and closer acquaintance with Susan Anthony had to wait a more propitious moment.

The moment came a few weeks later, when Elizabeth invited Susan to Seneca Falls to discuss a dream long cherished by a handful of progressive educators—the founding of a

People's College, to which women would be admitted on an equal footing with men. The project proved too far in advance of the period to be a success, but the conference brought together for the first time a young and gifted trio: the dynamic, brilliant Elizabeth Cady Stanton; Lucy Stone, friend of Garrison and at this time mainly an abolition speaker, whose silver voice worked miracles of persuasion; and Susan B. Anthony who was to become the most towering figure in the Movement for Woman's Rights.

It was Susan's first real meeting with the other two. She knew them chiefly through the unflattering publicity given them in the newspapers. Independent Quaker that Susan was, she remained stubbornly unconvinced, despite all Elizabeth's arguments, that women needed the vote to obtain their freedoms.

A few weeks later, however, she was much nearer conversion. She brought back to Seneca Falls a tale of injustice which had a familiar ring to Elizabeth who had sat in on the London Anti-Slavery Convention of 1840. Invited with numbers of other women temperance workers to a mass meeting in Albany, Susan had risen during the proceedings to offer her say on a motion. She was curtly interrupted by the chairman.

"Our sisters were not invited here to speak, but to listen and learn," he ruled pompously, whereupon Susan walked indignantly out of the hall with four other women delegates. But, alas, only four.

The majority of the Daughters of Temperance, shocked witnesses of her mutiny, remained sheepishly in their seats to listen as they were bid, and to learn no more than sheep usually learn.

After that, Susan readily admitted the need for a woman's movement and even conceded the possible need of the franchise, although she did not yet offer to join the ranks. Instead, she begged Elizabeth to help start a Woman's Temperance Society. She persuaded her also to preside at its first convention, and to deliver the opening address.

If Mrs. Stanton produced the eloquence, pleaded Susan, she herself would do the drudgery—gather statistics, collect an audience, arrange a meeting-place, and even introduce the speakers if she had to. Only let her be spared having to write a speech! Accustomed though she was to teaching, Susan suffered from the same diffidence all women felt in those days on a public platform. Most of all she distrusted her ability to marshal her arguments.

It was mortally important to the Woman's Cause at this time not to expose the inexperience of women speakers. Only too frequently their voices faltered and their manner was apologetic. Elizabeth hid her own nervousness behind native wit and impudence. But tied to her children at this period, the best she could do was to burn the midnight oil and furnish a rousing good argument for someone else to use.

So from now on, whenever Susan had an important speech to deliver before a Temperance group or, later, a woman's rights convention, Elizabeth supplied her the ammunition, charging it with the high explosive only she dared use.

Presiding now over Susan's newly created Female Temperance Society, and more concerned to save women than drunkards, she proposed a petition to the State legislature, to grant wives release from drink addicts.

The word "divorce" was as taboo then as was the word

"legs." Her bold use of it caused her five hundred lady listeners to hold up their hands in conventional horror. Whereupon Elizabeth, drawing on her knowledge of the slums near home, shocked them further by listing ironically the inconveniences of motherhood forced on a woman by a besotted partner, and the tragedy of sickly or mentally deficient children.

By this time she cared little for the uproar of public opinion. It appeared to be her destiny to explode the smugness of Victorian codes. When her fingers got scorched in the process, she was no longer surprised and little injured.

SEVEN

Having fired this latest shot, Elizabeth retired again behind a front of domesticity. The births of two girls and another boy within the next seven years added greatly to her responsibilities but could not curb her chosen purpose. Her daughters, arriving late, were a specially sacred trust. On them she would bestow all the privileges and freedoms denied her own generation.

Even the ordeal of birth was grist to Elizabeth's mill. While women of her world indulged in fainting spells and smelling salts, she attacked every phase of life full tilt, demonstrated that children could be brought into the world with comparative ease and very little professional assistance, and wrote articles on maternity and child care which punctured many a medical superstition of her day.

It was fortunate that mental and physical energies were so well matched. "My machinery is capable of running a long time," she wrote Liz Miller during a whirl of public and domestic duties, "unless," she added, "I burst my boiler screaming at boys, or explode from accumulated steam of a moral kind."

She had a threat it amused her to flourish under Susan's nose when the pressure to produce speeches and articles grew more than any one woman could bear. "As soon as you all begin to ask too much of me, I shall have a baby!"

And Susan, by this time up to her neck in the Woman's Rights meetings, knew better than to ignore the warning. How often had she not rushed down to Seneca Falls herself and forcibly taken over her friend's child-tending and pie-making, in order that she might free Elizabeth to work undistracted on some important convention address?

As soon as Elizabeth received a letter or a visit from the young Rochester Quaker these days, she could be sure of two things: that Susan was plotting fresh discomfiture for those gentlemen who desired a male monopoly on freedoms, and that some startling responsibility was about to descend on her own shoulders. Even so, resistance melted as soon as her friend stepped across her threshold.

The legislative business which kept Henry so frequently away in Albany was positively welcomed now, as the two talked endlessly through the night, before the blazing birch logs in Elizabeth's room. Those evenings, sealed in the hush of a sleeping house, spent in ardent, often fiercely whispered discussion, were unforgettable.

The pile of mending between them dwindled as they explored the theme of which they never wearied, weighing and debating how best to further the advance of Woman. Often they disagreed violently, but always by the time the fire's glow had died, dreams and plans were born which were to affect future generations.

Much as Henry Stanton liked and admired Susan, it was

not surprising, when he came home and found the two oblivious to all but their common obsession, that he struggled with a sense of injury. It was hard, he felt, that the minutes Elizabeth snatched from family cares were more often spent in writing for the Cause than in writing to him. Her children, she never neglected. But the Woman Movement was in its infancy too, desperately needing able adherents. So Henry, engrossed as he was in professional life away from home and remembering his own crusading, did not complain.

It was only human, however, to wish that his wife and Susan did not make so incomparable a team, especially when, as now, Susan turned up with a new and disturbing plan. It was high time, she insisted, that someone address the State Legislature on the legal disabilities of women, and who else but Mrs. Stanton had the ability?

For a woman to appear before the Judiciary was unprecedented. Elizabeth herself, knowing only too well the caliber of the men she would be facing, shrank from the test. Moreover, how find quiet for such a task in a house filled with boisterous young life? Only the nights were her own and they provided no time for research. Didn't Susan realize that to be guilty of inaccuracy before a group of attorneys was to court disaster?

Very well, replied Susan undaunted, and hastened back to Rochester to consult Judge Hays, who was a friend of their cause.

The Judge gladly agreed to furnish the statistics, insisting that Mrs. Stanton write and deliver the address. In this he was so strongly backed by William Henry Channing, another prominent feminist supporter, that Elizabeth had no choice.

Undeniably, a woman ought to plead the case for her own sex, and at the moment she was the one best fitted.

With the help of the data thus secured, and by dint of sitting up into the morning hours, she managed to shape her speech, in spite of the fact that home life had never piled up more strain and anxiety. An arrow shot by one of the boys injured her baby's eye during this time, and one of the maids fell ill.

The first draft of her speech was finally completed and approved by both Channing and Henry. But there remained two important factors. She must make herself heard clearly, to the last row of the Albany Senate Chamber, and she must appear entirely self-possessed, or the old claim that women were a failure in public life could not be denied. Each day Elizabeth practiced her speech in the musty solitude of her attic, making the rafters echo with her voice, until she was as prepared as she could possibly make herself.

But she had reckoned without her father. Judge Cady read the announcement of her hearing in an Albany paper and instantly concluded the worst. Of all her indiscretions, this was the culminating one. At the end of his successful career, to be shamed before his colleagues by the folly and conceit of a daughter!

Summoning all his lawyer's cunning, he sent a cordial invitation to Elizabeth to stop in Johnstown on her way to the hearing in Albany. Then, once she was under his roof, he threatened to disinherit her should she go through with her plan. Furious at the trick played on her, Elizabeth remained obdurate. He tried to bribe her. Elizabeth stood her ground. He had forgotten, she remarked, his advice to her in childhood, to carry the story of women's grievances direct to the lawmakers.

Silenced, her father's next move was diplomatic. Hadn't she better read him her address? He might save her much humiliation. She hardly understood, he felt sure, how difficult a thing she was attempting. Unwilling to refuse a reasonable request, Elizabeth began to read, though with trepidation. She dared not glance up. To encounter her father's scorn now, so soon before her performance in Albany, might unnerve her for good. Why hadn't she known better than to visit Johnstown before the ordeal?

She read on doggedly. The stillness in the room grew unbearable. Suddenly she could go no further. Forced to look up then, she saw that Judge Cady's face had softened. His deep-set eyes, fastened intently on her, were tear-dimmed.

No future triumph was ever to rival that moment's tribute, paid by a stubborn old man. Elizabeth picked up the thread of her address hastily, hiding her relief and astonishment, knowing that now she could face the Albany legislators with confidence.

Her hearing had been planned to climax the Woman's Rights Convention purposely held that year in Albany. Critics, well-wishers and mere curiosity seekers swelled the audience. Attracted also to the convention were people of note, including Ernestine Rose, famous Polish lecturer; the Rev. Antoinette Brown, the first ordained woman minister; Wendell Phillips and William Henry Channing.

When Elizabeth entered the packed Judiciary Chamber an expectant hush fell on the room, a silence so complete it almost stopped her heart. Appraising eyes followed her to her seat on the platform, took in the dignity of her full, erect figure in its simple black gown, marked the look of keen intellect, so like her father's. Among the legislators sat old associates of Judge Cady's, men who watched her sharply and thanked their stars their own womenfolk had no embarrassing endowment of brains.

It seemed to Elizabeth that behind their mask of impassive courtesy stood the collective antagonism of the whole judiciary. But in the rear of the Chamber sat that strong, unflinching soul, Susan—and with her a cohort of fellow workers, all waiting tensely, expecting her to show her old intrepidity. She was not going to fail them! On that note of defiance, she began her opening phrase.

"It is not enough that by your laws we are permitted to live and breathe,"—the cool irony of her attack took the Chamber by surprise—"to claim the necessaries of life from our legal protectors, to pay the penalty of our crimes; we demand the full recognition of all our rights as citizens of the Empire State."

Once started, her poised assurance grew, the atmosphere of the room changed subtly, to one of respectful attentive quiet.

Step by step she led her listeners through an impressive survey of the tragic predicament of women. Wives had no legal defense against husbands who pocketed their earnings and robbed them of their property. Hundreds were tied to dissolute partners with no possibility of release. Many mothers saw their sons apprenticed to gamblers and rum-sellers in payment of the father's debts. Daughters, for the same reason, could be bound out to owners of brothels, over their mother's entreaty.

"Would you could know the burning indignation that fills woman when she turns over the pages of your statute books, and sees there how like feudal barons you freemen hold your women," Elizabeth climaxed her plea. "We ask no better laws than those you have made for yourselves. We need no other protection than that which your present laws secure you."

When at length she sat down, a storm of applause greeted her. Judge Cady's friends were the first to give her enthusiastic assurance that their old colleague should be proud of his daughter.

Jubilant over the speech's success, Susan had fifty thousand copies printed and distributed, not forgetting to send one to each legislator, a delicate attention she might have omitted had she known none of them would give the address a second thought.

For the hearing which had cost her and Elizabeth untold effort, on which they had pinned so many hopes, fulfilled none of them. Like most novices, they had expected reform to come swiftly, whereas the hearing did little more than establish one woman's ability to compete with men in an untried field.

However, through this first failure and the many which were to follow (for they were to be outwitted and outmaneuvered repeatedly), women slowly learned the strategy of political warfare.

EIGHT

Six years later, Susan, who grew more determined with every defeat, urged Elizabeth to address the Senate Judiciary Committee again, this time to aid passage of greatly needed amendments to the Woman's Property Bill of 1848. Elizabeth's weeks of nerve-racking preparation for the earlier hearing, and its barren results, had left her with no special enthusiasm for a second attempt.

But Susan, insisting the odds were on their side now, triumphantly hauled her proof out of the old portmanteau, bulging with every conceivable data on women, which, as traveling salesman for the Cause, she carried everywhere.

"I have petitions to back you up this time, signed by hundreds of women in the state!"

"If Napoleon says cross the Alps, they are crossed," Elizabeth yielded with a wry shrug, and girded herself for another race with household interruptions, family emergencies and the flight of crowded hours.

Elizabeth's second hearing proved another brilliant personal triumph. Without the publicity it attracted, Susan's petitions would have gathered dust or been deliberately ignored. As it was, the State amendments were passed, and, because they are an amazing commentary on the position of married women at that period, they are worth a brief glance. They established in New York State a wife's ownership of her property, free from the control or interference of her husband.

They asserted her right to be gainfully employed, and secured her earnings against his appropriation.

They allowed her to sell or otherwise dispose of her property without consulting her husband, if he had deserted her, was insane, in prison, or an habitual drunkard.

For the first time, a married woman might sue or be sued in her own name. Any money recovered by such action was legally hers.

She was declared to be the joint guardian of her children with their father, with equal rights and privileges in regard to them.

Finally, a widow, whom marriage dispossessed of all, and whom the law granted only a third of her husband's estate, was given the same property rights at his death that he had when she died.

Married women in New York had now more freedom than any of their sisters in the Union, though they had done little enough to earn them. It had taken a three years' exhaustive canvass of the state and an unbelievable amount of persuasion on Susan's part, to get them to sign those petitions.

Elated over this first real gain, Susan and Elizabeth took it for granted that laws once passed are safe from marauders, an error for which they were to pay dearly.

During the Civil War they both dropped their crusading

temporarily to help the Negro, and in Albany were men waiting just such an opportunity to revoke the clause giving mothers equal guardianship over the children, and that protecting the rights of widows. Other amendments to the Bill were left untouched, but the two most shameful practices they had abolished were again sanctioned.

The setback determined Susan to work for enfranchisement more zealously than ever. The power behind the vote alone would protect women's gains. How right Mrs. Stanton had been about that—and yet how impossible to hold her steadily to that one goal!

For Elizabeth Cady Stanton had not one wagon, but a whole caravan hitched to her star—side issues of the woman's cause, all driven with equal skill and recklessness, and most of them colliding with popular conventions.

Susan, just as intrepid but harnessed to burdens of organization no one else would bear, supported and defended her friend unfailingly. Only once, and much later, when Elizabeth's pace threatened to upset the gingerly balanced suffrage apple cart, carrying all their hard-won political gains, did she cry caution.

For the most part, Elizabeth crusaded for woman's advance in the way which suited her best, as a free lance. Her articles, ranging from home to politics, were beginning to waken a hitherto spineless and apathetic sisterhood. A bracing tonic to Mrs. Bloomer's *Lily*, they were now in great demand for other women's periodicals, and the New York *Tribune*, owned by Horace Greeley, who was feeling cordial at the moment to Elizabeth and her projects, printed everything she cared to send.

About this time also, Providence sent Elizabeth the long-delayed blessing of a capable housekeeper. Amelia Willard was a liberal-minded Quaker and stout supporter of the Woman's Cause, who considered it her mission to take charge of the Stanton children while their mother livened up some of the meetings Susan was always organizing.

This arrangement released Elizabeth to speak at every important woman's rights convention. The one held in New York City in 1860 was the largest yet planned; a few fireworks would not be amiss. What better moment to re-open her fight for more liberal divorce practices? The issue had lain dormant since the day several years ago, when she had first exploded it in the midst of a Rochester convention.

At that time a number of Rochester ladies had gathered up their shawls and reticules and taken their immediate departure. Others, who had displayed an unseemly inclination to hear more, were firmly escorted to the door by their husbands.

But plenty stayed, for marital infidelity was a scourge as old as Eve, and the remedy, obviously, did not lie with the sons of Adam. It was time a woman did something about it.

Moreover, Elizabeth remembered that her speech had given a number of women in Rochester a little more courage to go on living. She never forgot those who pushed quietly through the crowd afterwards to press her hand. Among her acquaintances, she knew several like these whose lips were sealed, but whose story was written in their faces. Fine-grained, sensitive women who lived with degradation rather than abandon their children to the dissolute father who was their legal guardian.

An unhappy wife did not apply for divorce in those days. Besides the disgrace attached to it, she had no money of her own to pay a lawyer, unless she happened to live in the Empire State. The best any woman could hope for, who left her husband's "bed and board," was to throw herself on the charity of relatives, and even this involved her in scandal to which she preferred almost any humiliation.

"Wedlock" was an apt term for a union which could never be dissolved, no matter how unbearable its conditions; a coercion of men as well as women. Elizabeth had seen at close range the effects of a loveless marriage needlessly embitter the lives of a sister and brother-in-law.

Finally, she intended to protest the double standard of morality for the two sexes, and urged an equal penalty for its breach. At present, social laws and censure were relentless toward the woman offender, but a man could sow his "wild oats" unpunished.

Feeling she needed some support, Elizabeth appealed to Lucy Stone just before the New York Convention. Surely Lucy, who had suffered martyrdom in her stand for equality of the marriage vows, and who had agreed with her on all these points, would uphold her publicly?

But Lucy sent back a carefully worded reply that committed her to no action, and which led Elizabeth to believe in her support.

The subject of divorce needed to be presented with extreme delicacy, if not with prayer, Lucy intimated, and this, considering the eggs and epithets which had been hurled at her for suggesting a few changes in the marriage rites, was an understatement.

"God touch your lips if you speak on it," she ended with understandable fervor.

What really issued from Elizabeth's lips at the convention held her listeners spellbound; a dispassionate summary of marital grievances, which for frankness placed her more than half a century ahead of her times. Stripped of the pious humbug and the prudery which had surrounded the subject all these years, she handed it without apologies to a mixed audience, for open debate. No one had dared such a thing before.

One by one, Elizabeth's fellow speakers shook off their fascination and amazement while she introduced one unsuitable topic after another. Now it was lost women, the very dregs of society, for whom she was pleading more humane treatment.

The Rev. Antoinette Brown was the first to rise in protest, as soon as she could make herself heard above the applause which burst involuntarily from the audience. The acid resentment of Christian clergymen who had opposed a woman's election to "the cloth" had no doubt much to do with her orthodox views. She had no mind to jeopardize women's chances in the pulpit by approving what would most certainly be denounced as a doctrine of "free love."

Garrison and Wendell Phillips, old champions of woman's rights though they were, reacted somewhat like men who have not been consulted, as indeed they had not. Their impulsive friend Mrs. Stanton was too prone to act on her own initiative. Did she think such an unconventional departure was likely to advance the Woman's Cause, already staggering under a weight of public odium and ridicule?

Phillips moved to have the whole incident stricken from

the records. Divorce was an issue which affected men as well as women. It had no place in a convention called for woman's rights.

To Elizabeth's surprise and no little hurt, Lucy Stone did not enter the controversy at all, reluctant, no doubt, to add any more fuel to the fire. Later on when challenged, she sided with Phillips. No one who knew Lucy could accuse her of cowardice. Believing devoutly in the sacredness and permanence of the marriage vows, she had taken exception to Elizabeth's claim that incompatibility was a valid reason for divorce.

Ernestine Rose, always a spirited speaker, came impetuously to Elizabeth's defense however, and Susan, who could be inspired at times, leaped to her feet with a withering contradiction of Phillips' statement that divorce had no place on the agenda.

By this time the fat was frying merrily, and reporters at the convention, elated over the squabble, gave it a sensational twist. Protests, abuse, distortion of her statements, and a few heartening letters of congratulation fell in a mixed shower on Elizabeth's unchastened head.

"One word of thanks from a suffering woman outweighs with me the howls of all Christendom," was her answer to the uproar raised by the clergy.

NINE

Only one phase of the situation was deeply disturbing to Elizabeth. She had unwittingly started the first open rift in the ranks of feminist leaders. Events which were to lead to a definite break now followed in the wake of the Civil War.

At this time abolitionists who had been the original agitators for woman's rights were drawn back into antislavery work. Many, like Lucretia Mott, had devoted their lives to liberate the Negro, before they saw the need to free women. It was natural that the slave should have a prior claim on them now the Negro's struggle had come to a climax.

Elizabeth herself talked Susan out of holding any more women's conventions until the Negro's fate should be decided. Nobody had time or interest for anything but the war, while almost every family had some man involved in the fighting. One of Elizabeth's boys ran away from home to join the army. For her, there were days of tension and anxiety until his age was discovered and he was discharged. In the midst of such personal strains the old home in Seneca Falls had to be abandoned. Henry Stanton had found a position in New York City which gave him the larger income he badly needed to support his family. Her days of comparative quiet and obscurity were over for Elizabeth.

She did her share of knitting and bandage-rolling, but for a woman of her ability in stirring times, that was hardly enough. Together with Susan, she joined the antislavery forces in New York and traveled the state speaking for emancipation. However, talk only inflamed public feeling. In Albany, the Mayor, a believer in freedom of speech, mounted the platform with them, gun in hand, to preserve order. But elsewhere, mobsters shouted them down and threatened to burn the roof over their heads.

In these early days of the war, Elizabeth was bitterly critical of Lincoln. There was nothing about the Illinois rail-splitter, with his high-pitched Western drawl, that reassured abolitionists or Democrats, used to the suave oratory of Eastern tradition.

His ungainly body and ugly, sorrowing face were targets for every cartoonist. Even his Cabinet talked about his inept humor and lack of official dignity. While his personality was no gauge of a man, his policies were, and Lincoln had sworn he would save the Union at the expense of the Negro—if he had to. This Elizabeth could neither understand nor forgive.

Later she frankly admitted misjudging him when the years revealed a Lincoln of towering size.

With the close of the Civil War, she and Susan lost no time resuming their fight to enfranchise women. But now they were faced by the astounding desertion of Wendell Phillips, recently elected head of the Abolition Society.

The Negro had been freed indeed, but that was only the

first step. He must be granted full citizenship to protect his new liberties. Only the vote could insure them. Few contested this point; certainly not Elizabeth and Susan, only too aware that freedoms gained can be as quickly lost. But they did insist that woman's need for the franchise and the Negro's were of equal importance.

Greeley, Garrison, Frederick Douglass, Thomas Higginson, Phillips—all who had once encouraged them to demand the vote—were now urging them to drop it for an indefinite time. To unite the two issues, argued Phillips, was to retard the Negro's chances, riding a favorable tide since the war. Enfranchisement of women was likely to be opposed for years to come, but the Negro's hour was clearly here.

"May I ask just one question," Elizabeth flung back at him, "based on the apparent opposition in which you place the Negro and woman? Do you believe the African race is composed entirely of males?"

To all intents and purposes the answer was "Yes," as Elizabeth soon learned. The Fourteenth Amendment to the Constitution, passed a year later, defined voters specifically as "male citizens." By one small word in the second clause of this amendment, women were neatly eliminated.

Susan and Elizabeth were fighting mad. In the crusade to end slavery none had pleaded so eloquently for the Negro as women, none had been so dishonored and vilified for their stand. Lucretia Mott, the Grimké Sisters and those who followed them had risked much more than men when they became abolitionists. Was their reward to be put off, now they were no longer needed? Were women to be treated like inconvenient creditors?

Because Phillips and the majority deserting the woman's cause were Republicans, Elizabeth and Susan appealed to influential friends in the Democratic Party to back an amendment granting both women and the Negro the vote. But the men who consented were first of all Democrats, mainly interested in opposing and embarrassing the Republican administration and their efforts soon petered out.

TEN

At this moment news came from Kansas which sent Elizabeth's and Susan's hopes skyrocketing. In that pioneer Western state, people were considering just such an amendment to enfranchise both Kansas women and Negroes. Lucy Stone and her husband had just returned from a speaking tour there in support of the bill, and had brought home an enthusiastic report. Kansas folk were the most progressive they had ever met! Kansas would lead the country in reform, pave the way for a new order! Go out, they said to Susan and Elizabeth, and finish the job we have begun.

Elizabeth and Susan caught fire at once. The Stanton children were almost all at a responsible age now, and Amelia Willard was still in charge. It was terribly important to give woman suffrage a boost in the one state likely to give it a chance, and Elizabeth, who had made hundreds of speeches but had never been free for the tireless kind of campaigning Susan did, was eager to test herself on the road.

It took hardihood to embark on a lecture tour of the Midwest in the 1860's especially for Elizabeth, well past her youth and in middle life. The luxury of railroad travel in those days included liberal showers of cinders and dust, hours of jogging over rough roadbeds, inadequate sleep, hastily swallowed meals. For itinerant speakers it meant also stepping onto a platform at the other end of the ride, looking immaculate and well-fed, however grimy and supperless; dishing up for a new audience each night the same glowing enthusiasm and eloquence.

Seeing them off under the blackened shed of the old railway terminal in New York, Henry Stanton wished them a pleasant trip of it—a bit ironically, perhaps, although he hadn't a doubt they would return as undaunted as ever. It must sometimes have come over Henry that he had no one but himself to thank for exposing Elizabeth in youth to the contagion of Lucretia Mott and Garrison.

On the train, Elizabeth and Susan settled down to their notes and tracts, jammed into Susan's now battered handbag, and to the thrill of shared adventure which the two of them never lost. They were headed for a few things they had not foreseen: the dreadful squalor of prairie settlements; dirt, fleas, vermin, the horrors of pioneer cooking; and a meeting with George Francis Train.

The most fantastic incident of the trip was their friendship with this notorious character.

George Francis Train was an eccentric with a dash of genius, who had made a fortune in adventurous enterprises. He had Irish wit and a flair for crusades. When he offered himself to the woman suffrage campaign in Kansas, its handful of organizers was too thankful for any kind of help to mind the vaudeville act he put on.

Susan invited Train to tour the state with them, a plan

which horrified all their staid friends in Boston and New York. The movement could scarcely afford to be mixed up with a three-ringed circus!

Mr. Train might be unconventional, Elizabeth replied tartly, but at least his loyalty to the cause was not tainted with politics. She forgot to mention his lavendar kid gloves and sky-blue suits trimmed with brass buttons, but she let everyone know he was a gentleman, neither "smoking, chewing, drinking nor gormandizing!"

There was no denying that Train's platform antics swept audiences off their feet, that his gift for epigram was dazzling.

The peak of his showmanship in Kansas came at the end of the tour, when he announced the birth of a weekly paper for the Woman's Rights Movement, christened it *The Revolution*, made Susan its proprietor, Elizabeth its editor-in-chief, and furnished it with money and the slogan, "Men, their rights and nothing more; women, their rights and nothing less."

When Susan and Elizabeth were able to believe what had happened to them they were jubilant. Critics at home would admit now that a little flag-waving and band music had done the Cause no harm! For years everyone had acknowledged the need of a periodical for the Movement; for years everyone had despaired of being able to raise enough interest or funds. What did it matter that the vision and the greenbacks were provided by an odd personality?

The fulfillment of their dream did much to console the unregenerate pair for the failure of the woman suffrage bill in Kansas. As Henry Stanton had guessed, they came home undefeated, if possible with more confidence and drive, gained from their tour with a flamboyant Irishman.

They had need of it. Instead of felicitations, they got a cold welcome from the fold. Everything about *The Revolution* made their old associates shudder—its sensational title, aggressive slogan, and its two sponsors, Train and a none-too-fastidious business partner of his. Elizabeth and Susan were accused of letting charlatans ruin the Cause.

Garrison, Phillips, the Blackwells, and most of the other Boston leaders promptly washed their hands of *The Revolution*, whereupon it became a private venture. Its owner and editor-in-chief wasted no time resenting the reception given it. They were too busy finding offices and a printer, winning subscribers, persuading advertisers and hunting up writers for their columns. They had never been a more effective team. Elizabeth did not hide her satisfaction that now she was accountable to no one but herself and Susan.

It had begun to seem to her as if the Cause was being run by a select coterie, so encircled had the movement become with Beechers and Stowes, Higginsons, Tiltons and Phillipses. Real victims of the law were not protected by privilege and influence.

In *The Revolution* Elizabeth had printed the true facts about a servant maid imprisoned for infanticide. The girl had been seduced by her employer and thrown into the street. Friendless and without money, she had sought shelter in an unheated attic, where her child was born and immediately died.

Yet champions of woman's rights objected to Elizabeth's public defense of the mother, because it dragged the Movement through a notorious scandal. For Hester Vaughn and all her forlorn sisters on whom society was merciless, and for the great host of laboring women who received starvation wages, *The Revolution* was going to crusade tirelessly.

But the paper almost went on the rocks as soon as it had been launched. On a visit to England, Train embraced the Irish Cause so enthusiastically that he was clapped into prison for a year, leaving Elizabeth and Susan holding an empty purse.

By initiative and energy such as only Susan was capable of, it stayed alive for two more years; long enough to wage a losing but vigorous fight against the Fifteenth Amendment to the Constitution, which enfranchised the Negro and left woman to struggle on unaided.

It was during the months of violent disagreement over this sole issue, that Elizabeth severed her connection with the Boston faction led by Phillips and Lucy Stone.

Both sides supported enfranchisement of the Negro; both claimed the same right for women; but to give priority to an illiterate group, while women remained in a voteless class with insane people and criminals, was too much for Elizabeth and Susan. If women were not to be included in the Fifteenth Amendment, they would oppose it.

The two were promptly accused by the Boston suffragists of wanting to keep from others what they could not get for themselves. To Lucy their stand seemed ungenerous, to men abolitionists it was unworthy of woman's role of noble self-abnegation, which, Susan pointed out, was also a fatuous and thankless one.

Whether women would have benefited in the long run by being enfranchised with the Negro is a question that will never be answered to everyone's satisfaction. Comparatively few women at that time wanted the vote, or were adequately prepared to use it, an argument which applied equally to the Negro. In the half-century which was to elapse before woman suffrage became a constitutional right, the movement had time to develop from a small band of pioneers into an overwhelmingly large group of better educated, more awakened citizens.

Persuaded, with some justice, that so long as men were influential in the crusade, women might wait indefinitely for the vote, Elizabeth, Susan and their supporters founded the *National* Woman Suffrage Association, whose rules required that only women should direct its affairs. Elizabeth Cady Stanton became the first President, an office she filled for the next twenty years.

Whereupon the New England group, led by Lucy Stone, also organized, calling themselves the *American* Woman Suffrage Association. A last-minute effort of reconciliation failed, perhaps fortunately. The clash of temperaments between militants and conciliators, between those who will not compromise and those who seek a middle ground, is rarely resolved in mid-battle. Only after the dust of conflict settles is it plain that both sides served.

Although Elizabeth was the nominal leader of the new suffrage association, the burden of its management fell on Susan. Literally as well as figuratively, from now on Elizabeth went her own way. She was very tired of being told that her ideas were rash and incendiary and her leadership dangerous. All those charges were ancient history, as old as the Seneca Falls Convention and her lone stand for the franchise. With driving intellect and great physical energy to whet her impatience, it was a wonder she had not chosen independent action sooner.

Family considerations were a factor in her present decision. Henry's income had increased since his move to the city, but not enough for the adequate education of seven children, all of whom, their parents agreed, must go to college.

ELEVEN

It so happened that lecturers were in great demand at this time, especially in the newly settled West, turning eagerly from the culture of livestock to that of the mind. Already well known through her Kansas campaigning, Elizabeth was one of the first speakers to be engaged by the New York Lyceum Bureau. Everything about the offer made it acceptable. The fee was high, her need to earn imperative, and here was an unparalleled chance to spread the gospel of free womanhood where prejudices were few.

Elizabeth Cady Stanton in her middle fifties was in top form. The plump figure had grown imposing, the thick hair, piled high in a mass of white curls, made a royal crown. Good nature, a rich sense of humor and deviltry, were some of her assets; and no one who laid a trap for her tried it a second time.

Before a committee of prominent legislators, Horace Greeley once thought he had her cornered. "The ballot and the bullet go together. If you vote are you ready to fight?" he asked.

"Yes, we are ready to fight, sir, just as you did in the war, by sending our substitutes," came the stinging rejoinder.

Annually, from October to June, Elizabeth stumped the West until her children were out of college. It was an assignment covering twelve years, at a period when travel and accommodations all through Western regions were primitive. In winter, lecturers had to surmount awful cold, flood and storm, but Elizabeth held an unbeatable record for keeping to schedule.

Once in Iowa, all transportation being blocked by raging blizzards, Elizabeth hired a sleigh with a skilled driver. Wrapped to the eyes in buffalo robes, she drove six hours through drifts and sub-zero temperatures, to her next appointment. She was well over sixty then. To her, a crowded hall was enough reward for such a feat, and her meeting a few days later with two other lecturers, both men. This pair had let three weeks' worth of engagements slip through their fingers, waiting for the roads to be opened.

One of them was General Kilpatrick of Civil War fame, whose main theme was his march to the sea with Sherman.

"And yet," exclaimed Elizabeth, "you couldn't march in an emergency across the state of Iowa!"

Toward the end of those twelve years, she pushed herself wearily but gamely through the familiar routine.

"Two more months, containing sixty-one days," she counted what was left of her tenth circuit, "I must pack and unpack my trunk sixty-one times; pull out the black silk trail and don it; puff my hair and pin on the illusion ruffling round my spacious throat, sixty-one more times; shake hands with sixty-one committees, smile, try to look intelligent and interested in everyone; and endeavor to affect a little spring and briskness in my gait in order to avoid giving the impression that I am seventy; when in reality I feel more like crawling than walking."

Among the men and women lecturing on the Western circuit in those days, none raised more controversy or provided more entertainment. Her ability to deal with smart alecks became legendary.

In Lincoln, Nebraska, a puny, bowlegged man had baited her repeatedly during the question period after the lecture. Finally he picked up a chair, and setting it directly in front of hers, made several mocking insinuations about woman's chief duty to increase the race.

"My wife has presented me with eight beautiful children," he wound up facetiously. "Isn't that better lifework than exercising the right of suffrage?"

Surveyed at close range, he was no Adonis. Elizabeth gave him the careful inspection he had invited, and then remarked: "I have met few men in my life worth repeating eight times."

Adding constantly to her lectures, she did a good deal of writing on trains, between destinations. Divorce, unwanted motherhood and coeducation were subjects the hardy Westerner seemed able to face without wincing. For Sundays she prepared suitable lectures, used whenever some unwary minister invited her to speak. One discourse was on the ruling queens of the Old Testament; another discussed Bible passages supporting the equality of male and female; the last was a survey of the clergy's attempt, through the ages, to subdue and belittle women.

"I have never let an occasion slip to storm a pulpit," Elizabeth admitted, "though the storm generally breaks after I have taken a back seat."

Humdrum organized work to liberate women was temperamentally impossible to her. She felt justified in furthering the Cause in her own unorthodox way, particularly as she never shirked the writing assignments loaded on her as President of her suffrage association.

Summers too, during this busy stretch of her life, were largely devoted to suffrage activities, her most notable service being her address before the Senate Committee in Washington, when a Sixteenth Amendment to the Constitution was proposed, resolving that "the rights of citizens of the United States to vote shall not be denied or abridged . . . *on account of sex.*"

Back in Boston, the American Woman Suffrage Association refused to support this federal amendment, affirming their preference for state-by-state enfranchisement of women. Elizabeth's appearance before the Senate Committee established a precedent. From that time on, the question of woman's enfranchisement was given an annual hearing in the capital.

TWELVE

It was between her Western tours that Elizabeth and Susan began work on the first volume of their *History of Woman Suffrage*. Elizabeth welcomed this chance for companionship again.

Buried in organization duties, Susan was impossible to see these days, unless a project of the kind demanded her presence.

"The New York *Sun* has an article about you and me 'having dissolved partnership,'" Elizabeth complained. "Have you been getting a divorce in Chicago without notifying me? I consider our relations are to last through life."

The truth of the matter was, Susan was irked by Elizabeth's absence the major part of every year and her refusal to be harnessed to the Movement, and Susan said so bluntly. The two no longer saw eye-to-eye on a lot of things. With the wisdom of tried friends, they neither ignored this regrettable fact nor pursued it too far.

Their *History*, otherwise, would never have been completed. The task of sorting thousands of yellowing letters, clippings and documents was bad enough; they also had to agree on the running comments with which Elizabeth was to knit all this material together.

Susan was the soul of exactness; Elizabeth, left to herself, swept aside encumbering details to interpret the Movement. Snipping and pasting, scribbling and arguing, they faced each other across a big table, each sticking to her point and getting in the other's way. Susan's absent-minded habit of dipping her mucilage brush into the inkpot was the least of their conflicts.

The large, sunny library at Tenafly, strewn with papers, dictionaries and statute books, was their workshop. No one else entered that chaos, or wanted to. Labors started serenely each morning, in the peace of complete absorption. Then a disagreement would halt work. Soon it was audible through closed doors. "Aunt Susan and Mother are at it again," the household had sometimes to explain.

By afternoon, disputes had risen to a heated pitch. Thump! A book was slammed shut, a chair rasped across the floor, the library doors flew open, and out stalked one or both historians to cool their tempers in solitude.

Evening always found them pacing the lawn arm-in-arm, deep in the most amicable discussion.

"They never explain, nor apologize, nor shed tears, nor make up, as other people do," Margaret Stanton described these mystifying reconciliations.

The first volume of the *History of Woman Suffrage* was finished and published, just as Elizabeth completed her final year of lecturing. It was a fitting climax to the most strenuous phase of her life. By that time the second volume was also well along, having received the able assistance of Matilda Joslyn

Gage as well as of Susan. Its publication followed hard upon the first.

A long-due vacation was now both desirable and justified. Harriot, the daughter closest to Elizabeth, wanted to earn a European degree, and Margaret, already married, was summering in France with her husband and baby.

After giant labors it felt strange to be released into the carefree atmosphere of tourist life. In the pleasant gardens of the convent at Toulouse where they stayed, Elizabeth gave herself up to lazy delight in the change. It was diverting to be idle while Harriot studied, to hope the Spartan convent diet would reduce her girth, since it added nothing to enjoyment; to offer the docile nuns a mild dose of emancipated woman, and to watch the progress of Harriot's romance with the young English student, William Blatch.

Autumn brought Harriot's marriage in England, and Elizabeth stayed on to see her daughter settled in her new home. Later Susan arrived for a richly deserved vacation herself. For two comrades so long in harness together the whole holiday episode was a lark. There were rich contacts in London, besides meetings with English suffragists whose speeches (before the days of Mrs. Pankhurst) were carefully edited not to offend the "dear Queen." Such innocuous crusading made Susan and Elizabeth glad to get home to hard-hitting American tactics.

The onerous job of bringing their *History* up to date with a third volume awaited the two as soon as they returned. They were heartily tired of the work by this time. Its tedium, Susan's itch to campaign, Elizabeth's to get on with her writing, all made the work an ordeal. They would have welcomed nothing so much as a daily wrangle but this stimulating pastime had become almost obsolete now the work was well organized. Both were frankly impatient to go their separate ways long before the final T was crossed.

THIRTEEN

Elizabeth's articles, full of revolutionary matter, were appearing in many leading periodicals when her seventieth birthday caught up with her. Americans paused, as they have a habit of doing even in the midst of a fray, to salute a veteran opponent. *The New Era,* a woman's magazine, devoted a whole issue to her, and all over the country conventions and meetings celebrated her contribution to woman's advance.

Henry, that same year, came in for his share of glory, with the publication of his book *Random Recollections,* and a birthday dinner given him by the New York Press Club. It was a time for evaluating the good life shared together, each pursuing his chosen vocation.

With the turn of another year, while Elizabeth was in England visiting Harriot again, Henry died very suddenly.

She had less desire than ever now to come home and get trapped in the vortex of Susan's plans. Harriot and the babies were a great solace, and life in England, free of the pressures she could not escape in America as a national leader, flowed in an easier tempo. If she chose to dabble in spiritualism, the latest craze, who was there to remind her it might injure the Cause? Abroad she could view the Movement with more cynicism and fewer twinges of conscience. What with greater leisure and freedom, the time had come for the book refuting false religious doctrines, which she had always promised herself to publish. Up to now the Scriptures had been interpreted from a purely masculine angle. Men had ranked themselves as Deity's primary creation, giving woman second place in the divine plan. Men had conceived of the Creator as Father, whereas the complete Godhead must be Father-Mother, if the twenty-seventh verse in the first chapter of Genesis was to be credited. Another theological belief which had retarded woman was the theory of Eve's guilt and connivance with the serpent. Until this and many other basic superstitions were corrected, women would continue to believe in the inferiority of their own sex.

But for a project of this sort she needed the authority of scholarship and the collaboration of Bible students. Elizabeth's first step was to invite women fitted for such a task. To her chagrin many declined. Knowing the whole denominational field would raise an alarm, they were not going to add to any such bonfire as Mrs. Stanton proposed to light.

She had forgotten also to reckon with Susan.

"Leave the Bible alone," ordered Susan. "Once we get the vote, sectarian opinion will come around of itself." Later, Susan refused to jeopardize a suffrage campaign in California, by circulating either Elizabeth's Bible literature or Frances Willard's prohibition tracts.

"I have been pleading with Miss Willard for the last three months to withdraw her temperance invasion of California this year. Now don't you propose a 'Bible' invasion!"

"Always harping on that one theme of enfranchisement," sighed Elizabeth, who had originated it. "There are a number of other tunes."

There the matter rested for a while, but Elizabeth persisted. It took more than Susan and more than a movement's solid opposition to stop her, once she was convinced. Here and there a few intrepid women offered her their services, but the main portion of the commentaries she had to write herself. Her "Bible" was to be ten years in the making.

In the meantime, her attempt to remain safely in England, out of Susan's whirling orbit, was destined to be nipped in the bud. An international suffrage conference was to be held in Washington in the spring of 1888, to celebrate the fortieth anniversary of the now famous Seneca Falls Convention. It was out of the question, wrote Susan, already scenting refusal, that the author of the suffrage resolution should absent herself from this meeting. In their younger years together, had they not dreamed and hoped for just such an awaking on the part of foreign women?

But Elizabeth, suddenly facing a grim homecoming, without Henry on the pier, without a warm family welcome, recoiled. She was in no mood to grind out the "inspiring message" expected of her; the dreams and hopes of younger years were sawdust now; at seventy-three a winter crossing was anything but alluring. No, she wrote back, it was quite impossible for her to leave England.

Despondency—and a secret liking for comfort and leisure! Thus Susan summed up Elizabeth's frailties, wondering how she was to explain to the conference the absence of the woman they had come to honor.

For her own and everybody's sake, Elizabeth must be roused! Susan's rousing scorched the very paper she used, and caused her two sleepless nights of remorse. Ten days of anxious waiting. Perhaps she would never hear from Elizabeth again. Then—

"I am coming," said the brief cable from England. More between those two would have been superfluous.

Elizabeth arrived minus even a first paragraph with which to address the conclave, a twinkle of defiance in her shrewd old eyes. But Susan shut her into a room of their Washington hotel, placing a guard at the door. As in the days of youth when Susan baked the pudding while Elizabeth wrote, the address rolled out on time, with all the old smoothness and brilliance!

Many younger suffragists were enlisting in the movement now. Susan's campaigns, Lucy's persuasion, Elizabeth's fearless attacks were all shaping the future. The new crusaders were demanding an end to the schism which was still weakening the Movement. A move to unite was afoot. The merging of the two woman suffrage associations under the title *National American* took place before Elizabeth went back to England.

Mellowed by the years, all the old pioneers came to the big mass meeting. Probably no more notable gathering of headstrong zealots ever came together. The marvel is they did not immediately start fighting again. But for this occasion speeches were carefully edited. Only rarely a flash of caustic wit hinted an old feud.

Elizabeth was both touched and surprised to find herself elected President, an honor she accepted, only to relinquish two years later, when advancing years seemed to justify her withdrawal from active service.

She was seventy-seven when she made her last and most powerful appeal for woman's rights, before the House and Senate Judiciary Committees in Washington. The nation's lawmakers were genuinely impressed. They printed ten thousand copies of her address, a gesture they seemed to consider all-sufficient. Nevertheless, enfranchisement inched a trifle nearer.

One more visit to Harriot in England, and Elizabeth returned to New York City to stay. An injury suffered in a fall was to curtail her traveling from now on. On her eightieth birthday, she was given a tremendous ovation in the Metropolitan Opera House. New York newspapers, even those which were most consistently ridiculing woman suffrage, paid her reverent tribute.

As she stood, shaken, before the mob of six thousand cheering men and women, leaning on her cane and fighting back emotion, her snow-white head massive with the weight of years, no one would have believed that Elizabeth Stanton was about to launch the most explosive of all her attacks. A bare two weeks later, the first volume of the *Woman's Bible* startled the country.

The derision and criticism which greeted it, the fury of the clergy and the immediate repudiation of its title and contents by dismayed suffragists, would have killed any ordinary octogenarian. With the cynicism and detachment of age, Elizabeth merely waited for the storm to subside. Then she published her second volume.

The resentment of the whole suffrage organization, which

had to bear the brunt of this final "indiscretion" of Mrs. Stanton's, rallied Susan to magnificent defense of her old friend. She had been frankly impatient with the "Bible" project. Nevertheless she found it intolerable that younger workers, who had joined the Cause after the hardest fight was over, should pass judgment on the Founder of the crusade. Susan very nearly resigned from the Movement.

But the crisis passed and her indignation cooled. The *Woman's Bible* created a great stir, yet after the excitement abated, it was not widely read nor long remembered.

Elizabeth wasted no regrets over its oblivion. Truths once uttered, like stones cast in the sea, leave widening circles.

She had had her say, and now the sands were running out. She sensed it in the slowing of physical energies, in the panic of approaching blindness, hidden from those she loved. But her mind raced on. In between finishing her reminiscences, *Eighty Years and More,* she wrote constantly for the magazines; her correspondence up to the very end required a secretary.

She spoke frequently, and still went to the important suffrage conventions.

In her city apartment there was always room for Harriot's daughter, now finishing her education in the United States. "Queen Mother," all her grandchildren called her. She never grew old. Her wit made companionship sparkle, her wisdom was cheerful and courageous.

She was in her chair as usual one afternoon, when her heart quietly stopped. She had reached the venerable age of eighty-seven. Not many hours before, she had written an urgent plea to Theodore Roosevelt:

"Abraham Lincoln immortalized himself by the emancipation of four million Southern slaves. Speaking for my suffrage coadjutors, we now desire that you, Mr. President, who are already celebrated for so many honorable deeds and worthy utterances, immortalize yourself by bringing about the complete emancipation of thirty-six million women."

Elizabeth went out as she would have wanted to, pen in hand.

For a whole day, after the news reached her, Susan spoke to no one. In her closed room, alone, she sat remembering.

III

Lucy Stone

"A little, meek-looking, Quakerish body, with the sweetest and most modest manners, and yet as unshrinking and self-possessed as a loaded cannon."

Thomas Wentworth Higginson

"It is probably not generally known, that whenever a woman has accepted an offer of marriage, all she has, or expects to have, becomes virtually the property of the man thus accepted as husband: and no gift or deed executed by her between the period of acceptance and the marriage is held valid; for were she permitted to give away or otherwise settle her property, he might be disappointed in the wealth he looked to in making the offer."

Roper, *Law of Husband and Wife*
(Book 1, Chapter xiii)

ONE

The fields were blanketed in darkness. All that could be seen of the child, wrapped in her mother's old shawl, were her bare, twinkling feet on the cow path. It was very chill at that black hour just before dawn. An icy dew lay on the meadow grass and on the damp, hard-packed earth of the trail.

The little girl hugged the shawl tighter across her narrow chest. The tinkle of cowbells rose on the frosty air and the warm milky breath of the cattle, moving invisibly in the shadows ahead.

Up and up the steep path climbed, now over the pebbled surface of rocky ledges, now around some humped boulder which blocked the way. The stars softened, darkness melted into gray mist, fuzzy and thick as cat's fur. Here and there a tall pine reared its somber head above the morning fog. Except for the muffled hoofbeats of the herd, the earth was still.

Night and its phantom shapes held no terrors for Lucy, as they did for her older brother Luther, so it was she who drove the cows to pasture and watched the sun rise from the heights above Coy's Hill Farm. The sweep of valley and sky and the sunrise were brave glories for a child of eight to face every morning; they may well have stamped on her plain little face that rapt and shining look which never left it.

There was little enough at home to feed the hunger for beauty in Lucy Stone's young soul. Perhaps that was why she escaped so willingly at dawn to the music of birds and brooks, the sweet wild scents in the meadows and the daybreak. Through a long life of self-denying labor her love of nature remained intense, a never-failing comfort.

The habit of industry was formed early in Lucy, for on a New England farm, in 1818, the year of her birth, ancient methods of husbandry and home crafts were still practiced. Life was particularly hard on the women, upon whom fell the feeding and care of large households as well as the dairy work.

Nine children were born to Hannah and Francis Stone, and seven survived, an average record of birth and infant mortality for those days. Francis Stone's English ancestors had been among the earliest to seek religious freedom in the New World. Hardy and spirited colonizers, they had fought in the French and Indian Wars and the Revolution. Hannah's forebears, among whom were Forbes and Bowmans of Massachusetts, were more highly cultured.

Hannah's gentler breeding and woman's instinct caused her to dread the rough influences about her husband's tanyard for her children. She persuaded him to abandon the tannery for the farm on Coy's Hill in Massachusetts, and this seems to have been the only time she had her own way. Francis Stone, like many men of his day, was a despot in his own home. Vigorous and capable, he knew how to make his land produce, and he worked his women with equal thoroughness.

While there was always an abundance of everything on a farm, ready cash was a scarcity. In addition to their other chores, Lucy and her older sisters had each to sew a number of pairs of crude leather shoes a day. Lucy, being the fastest worker, was obliged to make nine. They were sold for the use of fieldhands or slaves and could be exchanged at the local stores for supplies, being valued at four cents a pair.

Hannah Stone not only made the clothing worn by the family but wove the material, while Lucy, deft and small enough to sit under the loom, separated the right threads and kept them from getting tangled. The little girl finished all her tasks neatly and quickly, and soon discovered that smartness earned women nothing on a farm but more labor.

Their day's work ended, men smoked and talked, their chairs tilted comfortably to ease their backs. She scarcely ever saw her mother sit, unless it was to weave or mend. The washing, churning and baking went on week after week without a break. She noticed, too, that no one's wishes were considered but her father's.

Hannah's protests at having to wash and cook for her husband's hard-drinking cronies, who settled down at her fireside for days at a time, fell on deaf ears. She sometimes wished she could drop in her tracks, but there was no time for dying on a farm. There was hardly time for bringing children into the world.

A few hours before Lucy was born Hannah had had to milk eight cows. A thunderstorm had threatened and all hands were busy in the fields, getting in the hay. No one questioned later whose emergency was greatest, Farmer Stone's or his wife's, except the obstinate young daughter born of her mother's resentment.

Lucy's anger could be a tornado. Rushing after a teasing sister one day, she caught a glimpse of her face in a mirror. Its white fury reminded her of a murderer's. Appalled, she turned and fled from the house. Dusk fell before she came out of hiding. With queer strength for a child, after that she held her tongue and her temper. No one ever suspected out of what depths of self-knowledge Lucy's gentleness grew.

In Farmer Stone's house there were only a handful of books besides the Scriptures. Lucy pored over the Bible as soon as she could read. She was not too young to have made up her mind about a good many things. She knew, for example, that she was never going to be the sort of wife her mother was— meek, resigned to her husband's unreasonable demands. But reading the story of Adam and Eve one day, she came upon a Bible verse which terrified her: "Thy desire shall be to thy husband, and he shall rule over thee."

Holy Writ was law, therefore women had no choice in the matter. She pondered the verse a long time. What she knew of her mother's life made its meaning intolerable. She came to the conclusion that it was better to die now, before such slavery could be imposed on her.

If dying had been simple as stepping out into the dark, Lucy would have gone as fearlessly as she went to pasture the cows; but how did one stop living?

"Is there anything that will put an end to me?" she asked her mother, and busy Hannah, who only half-listened to most questions, paused at this one.

When she understood the child's trouble she could only

repeat what she had been told herself. All women were under the curse of Eve. All women bore it patiently. Hannah's explanations were no comfort; all they did was to plant the first seeds of doubt in Lucy's logical young mind. The Bible was a translation, that much she knew from the inscription on the flyleaf. Perhaps the translators had made a mistake. Anyone who learned the "original tongues" could find out what the Scriptures meant for himself. To put an end to oneself seemed less sensible than to study Greek and Hebrew, and with this decision Lucy's growth out of a limited environment began.

She had always been an eager pupil and now she sensed a wide field of knowledge beyond the one-room school she attended. Fortunately for her, other schoolmates were demanding better instruction, and a college student was engaged to teach the district school. Even so, the path of learning was destined to be full of obstacles.

She soon saw that her mother was breaking under an impossible load, a fact which would remain invisible to her father until Hannah collapsed. Country graveyards were fairly well populated with tired farm wives, and Lucy thought that if anyone had to die of overwork on the Stone farm, it had better be someone more easily spared than her mother.

Having reached the mature age of twelve, it seemed to her quite logical to relieve Hannah of the huge household wash by doing it herself. Counting the hired men, there were always from ten to twelve people in the household. Eliza, the oldest sister, must already have left home, to marry and live on a farm of her own, perhaps; Rhoda taught school. There seems no other explanation why a child should have shouldered such backbreaking work unaided.

Laundry work was done outside in wooden tubs, and, before washing could start, water had to be heated on the stove and carried out in buckets. The farm day always began at dawn, and Lucy managed to get the clothes hung out before going to school, but she had to hurry back at recess to bring them in, and return to school for the afternoon. It meant, in all, four miles of daily trudging. She ironed evenings, and when the family went to bed she studied till she fell asleep over her books.

Sometimes too tired to stand up, the little girl stole to her room and dropped on her bed. But Hannah, watchful and worried, soon followed, whereupon Lucy got up hastily, pretending to put her room in order. By the time she was fourteen she had washed and ironed away most of the color out of her cheeks. It must have been at this time, when the rose complexion which was her one beauty failed to redeem her turned-up nose, that her father made his famous pun.

"Lucy's face is like a blacksmith's apron—it keeps the sparks away!"

"I wish I were plainer," Lucy flared back. "I don't want to marry."

Because his domination of Hannah was common practice it never occurred to Farmer Stone that his daughter might wish to escape her mother's fate. As for suitors, he must have been willfully obtuse. Besides her freshness and youth Lucy had a voice of unusual sweetness that was to work a powerful fascination on all who heard it.

She had one natural obsession, to be sure. She wanted a college education. Her father declared she must be "crazy," and Hannah had misgivings the wish was sinful. Learning beyond the elementary was only for boys, the future bread-winners. Whatever aid was possible went to them. Whenever Lucy needed a new textbook at school, she was told to use those her brothers had discarded. Whereupon she scoured the woods for berries and nuts and sold them to buy her own. The flavor of independence she tasted by this means, she found heady and much to her liking.

A discovery made when she was sixteen strengthened this unwomanly bent. The village sewing circle made shirts for theological students who were in need. Lucy, who was by this time teaching in the district school for a dollar a week, was an industrious member of the circle until a visiting pioneer educator, Mary Lyon, tried to interest the women in raising a fund for a girl's college. At the end of her talk, Lucy was considerably wiser.

Folding the man's shirt she had been making and laying it on the table, she made up her mind quietly not to finish it and hoped no one else would. She was through helping young men who were paid four times as much as was for teaching and who would earn their college fees long before she could.

Lucy had to prepare herself for college little by little; earning and studying by turns. Because women teachers were so poorly paid it was nine years before she had saved enough to go to Oberlin in Ohio, the only coeducational college in the country. She was twenty-five by then and the small hoard she had gathered was barely sufficient for her journey and to pay a half a year's tuition.

TWO

At Oberlin she swept and dusted the Ladies' Boarding Hall for three cents an hour, washed dishes, and taught whenever she had a chance, to meet expenses. Allowing herself fifty cents a week for food was meager fare, even in those days of low costs. By patching and darning she kept the few clothes she had brought with her neat and intact for the next four years.

The founders of Oberlin were two Presbyterian ministers whose liberal convictions, unique for clergymen in those times, embraced abolition as well as female education. The college was a station for the Underground Railway, a matter of ardent interest to Lucy who had hung a picture of Garrison in her room as soon as she arrived.

"Lucy says her prayers to it," laughed her college mates, and they were not far wrong.

Since the World Anti-Slavery Convention of 1840 in London, when the great abolitionist had championed the discredited women delegates, Garrison had worn for her a double halo. While Lucy was still in her teens, the antislavery crusading of Abby Kelley, the Grimké Sisters, Lucretia Mott and

Garrison had been sensational news even in so remote a spot as Coy's Hill. Their fight for emancipation and for women's right of free speech crystallized her own resentment against the domestic slavery she saw at home, and from then on against the enslavement of a race.

When she was asked to teach the fugitives quartered at Oberlin she very willingly consented, but the Negroes had other ideas, borrowed from the white man and rooted in tribal custom. Women were inferior to men. They had not risked everything for an education, to be cheated at their goal. As soon as she entered the classroom murmurs of dissatisfaction arose. Finally their spokesman explained the disturbance.

They wanted a man teacher.

Lucy reasoned with them goodnaturedly but without yielding. The important thing was to learn. Whether a man or a woman taught made no difference at all. She turned to the blackboard as though this unanswerable logic settled the matter, which it did.

With the same friendly reasoning she had once won over the leading bully in a class of unruly farm boys, who had thrown their last master out of the window. The Negroes were soon devoted students, eager to do her some service, and when a fire broke out in her dormitory rushed to the scene to rescue her belongings.

To Lucy, it took no unusual skill to handle people, just a little insight, and her own was crystal clear. At one time Oberlin authorities feared that a Negro student, who had become hopelessly infatuated with a white girl, might carry out his threat to throw himself down the college well. When all their efforts failed, they appealed to Lucy to bring him to his senses.

"Surely you don't want to ruin our drinking water," she put it to him reasonably. "Why don't you cut your throat instead?"—cold-blooded advice which worked an immediate cure.

Lucy had been in college two years when Antoinette Brown, the girl who was to become America's first ordained woman minister, came to Oberlin. She was years younger than Lucy, whose entrance had been delayed by having to earn her way; but the two were rebels of a kind and soon became close friends. They gave that firm guardian of female deportment at Oberlin, the Ladies' Board, plenty to talk about —especially Lucy.

"Miss Stone" had the temerity to remove her bonnet in church (because it gave her a blinding headache); she persuaded a sadly misguided professor to let her and Antoinette take part in a debate with the men students; she spoke at a meeting organized by her Negro students, and replied much too naïvely when called to account, that no, she had not felt in the least "out of place" on the platform with men (as the Ladies suggested she should have), because "I meet them every day in the classroom."

The Ladies' Board were unable to see why she objected to being one of a mute, obliging female audience provided for the men, who were the only students given practice in public speaking. She and Antoinette wasted no time over this point; they simply organized a small practice group of women for the same purpose, which met secretly, off campus, and was never discovered.

Another unseemly habit of Miss Stone's was her way of

probing in class every topic which concerned matrimony. Why, for example, had Montaigne remarked that women were "more sunk in marriage than men"?

The marriage contract, Professor Morgan had to admit, did not impose equal terms on men and women. A married woman not only relinquished ownership of her property and pledged obedience to her husband; but, in assuming his name, a wife gave up her entity, both socially and in law. This last humiliation had never been called to Lucy's attention before and it sank deep. It was at that moment that she made the resolve she was to keep all the rest of her life—never to surrender her name.

If Lucy, with her fresh complexion and round face, had not looked such a child; if, while flouting the clergy about bonnets, she had been irreverent; and if her relations with the "opposite sex" had held one grain of frivolity, the Ladies' Board would have known just what to do with her. But Lucy was a riddle, whom her distinguished and admiring old friend, Thomas Wentworth Higginson, once described as "a little, meek-looking, Quakerish body, with the sweetest and most modest manners, and yet as unshrinking and self-possessed as a loaded cannon."

Her final clash with authority came at graduation. The faculty had selected a few honor students, of whom she was one, to read their graduation essays at the exercises. When informed of the plan the Ladies' Board held up its collective hands in horror. Female students could neither sit on the platform with men, nor join with them publicly in the exercises. Their papers would be read for them by a member of the stronger sex, while they remained modestly in their seats.

This decree would have passed unchallenged, except that Lucy refused to write her essay at all, since she could not read it, whereupon every girl but one took the same stand, and two of the boys went on a sympathetic strike. The Ladies' Board did not yield, and neither did Lucy. Wearing her first new dress in four years, a homemade bombazine costing $4.66, she graduated with her appearance and her self-respect unimpaired.

THREE

She left Oberlin more determined than ever to remain single; with a fixation against marriage born of home memories, her own researches in college, and the admissions of Professor Morgan. That a wife exchanged her name for her husband's had become for Lucy a symbol of woman's whole subjugation. She was able to see now beyond what one domineering will did to a simple farm wife like Hannah. Marriage under existing laws and customs violated human rights.

In her earnest discussions with Antoinette Brown, as they roamed the Ohio countryside, she harped on that one theme. Antoinette thought it relatively unimportant whether a wife kept her name or not, when there were so many worse discriminations to fight. What could she do about it anyway, since no man would ever marry her if she refused to be Mrs. John Smith?

The two friends never did resolve the argument, and Lucy was just as unconvinced that Antoinette could ever succeed in her ambition to become an ordained minister. Lucy, however, was to keep her name in marriage and Antoinette was to achieve her goal, sooner than either could have believed possible.

Meantime, longing for home scenes and home faces after four years' absence, Lucy returned to a warm welcome at Coy's Hill. Bound to the same limiting superstitions, Hannah had changed little. She was sure no good was to come out of Lucy's headstrong plans for the future, just as she had feared it was not God's will that a girl should go to college.

Her father, on the other hand, had begun to respect his daughter's tenacity and spunk. Farmer Stone had even sent Lucy money in her third year at Oberlin, so that she need not take so much time from her studies to earn. One of her uncomplaining letters home had touched him. He answered it himself.

"When you wrote home that you had to get up at two o'clock to study, it made me think of the old tanyard where I had to get up at one and two o'clock. I little thought then that I should have a child that would have to do the same. I had to work early and late. I was hardly able to live. Let this suffice. There will be no trouble about money."

Lucy's present resolve not only to earn her living as a lecturer for abolition, but to emancipate women as well, pleased him no better than it did Hannah. Both objects would equally shock the neighbors. He seems to have made no protest; perhaps because it was so obvious by now that she would pursue her goal with quiet obstinacy, whether he liked it or not.

Had Lucy's sense of justice been less outraged in youth by tyrannies over Hannah, and the countless unfairnesses to her sex encountered in her struggle for an education, Liberty might not have worn for her so sacred a look. But her own ordeal was never to be forgotten. Whether the issue was Negro slavery or more subtle forms of bondage, wherever she saw human rights mocked and denied, she would come passionately to their defense.

Shortly after her homecoming, an older brother, William Bowman, whose liberal views were to lead him eventually to abandon a clergyman's career, loaned her his pulpit for a talk on women. This modest maiden speech, delivered in a small church a year before the Seneca Falls Convention of 1848, has become historic as the first public address on women's rights by an American woman. Lucy, unknown yet to Lucretia Mott or Elizabeth Cady Stanton, was blazing a lone trail.

Hannah suffered deeply over the mortifying event until her neighbors called to see how she was taking it. Then she fought Lucy's battle so ably that she converted herself! Crusty Yankee farmer that he was, Francis Stone kept his own counsel for a long time. Much later, when she was speaking near home, he slipped unnoticed into a rear seat of the hall. Hunched forward in his seat to avoid recognition, he was ready to sneak out as soon as his daughter's disgrace became too apparent. There he stayed, held by a power he did not comprehend.

Fervor lighted Lucy's plainness as by some law of compensation. Her voice, now muted and sweet, now full and silver-throated, chained her listeners to their seats. No more perfect instrument had ever been bestowed on a speaker. Farmer Stone crept quietly out toward the end, his ears tingling, not with shame, but pride.

Garrison's Anti-Slavery Society was quick to see possibilities in Lucy's voice and her native eloquence. They sought her out and engaged her to stump the New England districts for emancipation. Without any more preparation than that first simple talk to her brother's parishioners, she stepped before the deadly hostility of abolition audiences. One of the first antislavery meetings in which she had a part was broken up by a mob whose "demoniac yells" could be heard a mile away.

She was, as a matter of fact, most effective when there were no other speakers to break the spell she cast over an audience. Once her voice began spinning its silken magic, hecklers quieted, and generally allowed her to finish.

When churches or halls were found too small, abolitionists held open air gatherings on the outskirts of a community. In either case, announcements of the meeting had to be displayed in the town, and this took courage in itself.

Lucy posted her own meetings, hammering her signs on trees with tacks carried in her reticule and stones from the road. The first poster usually drew an army of young hoodlums who followed her up and down streets, taunting, flinging small missiles and pulling down her notices as soon as her back was turned.

However, she had not taught the roughest elements in farm districts without knowing how to preserve an unruffled front. She talked quietly as she went about her business, dropping a sentence now and then which piqued their curiosity. That black boys their own age were bought and sold in Southern markets like horses and cows brought the issue queerly close to home.

When she changed the subject to runaway slaves, her talk became enthralling.

Many communities had no interest at all in the slavery question. People came to her meetings to see the woman the Springfield *Republican* described as a "she-hyena," just as they would have gone to the circus to see a freak. They expected her to gesticulate wildly and hurl shrill invective. Women speakers were a brazen lot, and those sent out by the Garrison abolitionists must be crazy, since he was a dangerous crackpot.

When Lucy walked on the stage with her appealing smile, her quiet bearing and dress so plainly stamping her a lady, they were dumfounded.

For her ability to remain unperturbed through hoots, jeers and murderous assault, she had few equals. It was a common thing for her to face a rain of spitballs as soon as she stepped before an audience. Once a hymn book was flung at her head with such force it almost stunned her. On another night, in midwinter, icy water was trained on her from a hose thrust through a window. Lucy calmly reached for her shawl, wrapped it around her shoulders, and went on talking.

At an open air antislavery meeting on Cape Cod, the temper of the crowd seemed so dangerous that all the speakers, one after the other, vanished hastily from the platform. The only two left were Lucy and Abby Kelley's husband, Stephen Foster, a firebrand abolitionist of the same mettle from New Hampshire (not to be confused with the songwriter, Stephen Collins Foster).

Before either of them could get up to speak, Lucy saw the mob begin its advance.

"They're coming, Stephen. You'd better run for it," she warned him hurriedly.

Stephen no more than Lucy ever ran from danger. "What about you?" he protested, and with that the surging, yelling mass was upon them. Overpowered, Foster disappeared in the melee, and Lucy, suddenly deserted, looked up into the face of a towering ruffian with a club.

"This gentleman will take care of me," she suggested sweetly, taking his arm, and, too astonished for words, he complied. Reasoning calmly with him as he steered her out of the violence, she won his reluctant admiration and his consent to let her finish her speech. The platform was demolished by then, but he conducted her to a tree stump, rounded up the rest of the "gentlemen," and preserved order with raised club until she was through talking. Lucy gave the whole gang a piece of her mind, not neglecting to collect twenty dollars from them to replace Stephen Foster's coat, which in their gentlemanly exuberance they had split in two.

FOUR

Her later accounts of these stirring times were always modest. In her own opinion she had escaped the worst that could be perpetrated on a speaker. "I never had bad eggs thrown at me the way Abby Kelley did," she once assured a younger suffrage leader.

Her plight as a woman abolitionist, continually under attack because of her sex, not only fighting moral apathy toward slavery but battling for her own freedom of speech, made the two issues of parallel importance to Lucy. In the midst of anti-slavery work the other question haunted her perpetually.

She was in Boston at the time a statue, The Greek Slave, by Hiram Powers, was attracting much attention. When Lucy went to see it the exhibition hall was deserted. "There it stood in the silence," she wrote of it later, "with fettered hands and half-averted face, so emblematic of woman. I remember how the hot tears came into my eyes—"

The speech she had been scheduled to give that evening for the Anti-Slavery Society turned into a burning argument for woman's rights.

Tactfully the agent for the Society registered an objection

afterwards. Miss Stone had never been more spirited, but—hadn't she been engaged to speak for abolition?

Lucy did not answer for a minute. The point was entirely just. Then she said quietly, "Well, Mr. May, I was a woman before I was an abolitionist. I will not lecture any more for the Anti-Slavery Society. I must speak for women."

All her life she had been unconsciously approaching this decision. She reached it now without knowing how she was to support herself nor where the funds for this new work were to come from. Fortunately, Lucy was too valuable to the Garrison group. They persuaded her to continue lecturing for abolition on Saturday nights and Sundays. The antipathy of the clergy to woman's rights banned that ungodly subject from churches and halls during those hours anyway.

The modest income earned by this arrangement enabled Lucy to live—or, rather, barely to exist. She asked no fee for her talks on woman. An entrance charge might keep numbers of people away, and it was terribly important to her that all should hear. Lodging as she did in Boston in a garret, sleeping three in a bed with the landlady's daughters, for six and a quarter cents a night, held no terrors for her, and as for meals, Lucy had sustained life on a fly's portion before. She weighed under a hundred pounds, and the only part of her that grew stouter at this period was her courage.

After each lecture she passed a hat around. In this way she paid for placards and halls, but there was nothing left over for clothing. Eventually she learned that charging a small fee kept out the rowdies and scared away no one she wanted to reach, besides giving her a decent living.

Traveling up and down the country, educating women to

demand equal treatment and fairer laws, Lucy roused the apathetic and planted seeds of rebellion as far west as Missouri, while Elizabeth Cady Stanton and Susan B. Anthony were just beginning their crusade in New York.

On these trips she gathered an immense amount of material that became useful to later suffrage speakers. After each meeting numbers of women came up to confide in her. In this way she heard innumerable stories of marital injustice. Besides the sad and shameful accounts, many were funny and usual enough to be believed.

Two favorites dealt with the predicament of two widows left without adequate property rights. A man, who had imposed on a woman by an illegal marriage, died, and his relatives, begrudging the one-third of his estate which went to her, revealed the flaw in the marriage which invalidated it. The judge therefore advised the wife to send in a bill for her services for so many years, at so much a month, the ordinary wages paid a domestic servant. It took the entire estate to pay the bill, and the relatives got nothing.

The other widow had a right to the life use of one-third of her husband's real estate. She found it consisted of a plot in a cemetery, the use of which she could enjoy at death.

Lucy's intimate friendship with Garrison and Wendell Phillips began at the start of her feminist campaigning. Both men had always welcomed women associates in abolition work, and when in the year 1850, Lucy and eight sister members of the Anti-Slavery Society wanted to call a convention for woman's rights in Worcester, the two gladly counseled her and lent the prestige of their names to her crusade in Massachusetts.

They were to remain Lucy's warmest and most valued supporters. To her youthful hero worship of these seasoned reformers was now added enduring gratitude and loyalty. She shared with Garrison and Phillips, besides, a New England background in which Puritan influences were strong. It was no wonder that when conflicting policies split the suffrage movement, she chose the less militant, middle course, which was also theirs.

To this Worcester Convention Lucy invited as speakers all who had already declared themselves for woman's rights. Lucretia Mott was one of these. Elizabeth Cady Stanton, tied to family cares at the time, declined, but sent an enthusiastic message from Seneca Falls. Susan was not yet a convert. Two more years were to elapse before she joined the ranks and united the three most colorful figures of the Movement in friendship and purpose.

By then temperance, another issue of the hour, was pushing the woman's fight to the fore. Public censure of female speakers for abolition was mild compared to the frenzy of the clergy dominating temperance societies, who were determined to keep women off their own platforms. Their ire had already been sharpened by Lucy's friend of Oberlin days, Antoinette Brown, who was now preaching in a Congregational church and actually cherished the ambition to be ordained!

Ecclesiastical spite came to a head during a temperance convention in New York City, to which Antoinette was a delegate with credentials from two temperance societies. As soon as she appeared on the stage, a bedlam of protest broke out among her fellow saints. It continued without stop for three hours, while Antoinette, refusing to yield her place, remained on her feet. However, the argument whether or no a woman should be allowed to speak not only was not resolved, but raged on the next day and the next.

Horace Greeley reported the proceedings in the New York *Tribune* in five acid sentences:

> "This convention has completed three of its four business sessions and the results may be summed up as follows:
> "First Day—Crowding a woman off the platform.
> "Second Day—Gagging her.
> "Third Day—Voting that she shall stay gagged.
> "Having thus disposed of the main question, we presume the incidentals will be finished this morning."

During the same week, while bigotry was shutting up Antoinette in one quarter of the city, a woman's rights convention, organized by Lucy, was in session in another part of town, and was faring only a little better. Lucretia Mott presided over this gathering. Howls, catcalls and jeers produced such pandemonium that the meeting has gone down in history as the Mob Convention. Disregarding William Henry Channing's advice to adjourn, Lucretia replied calmly at the height of the uproar:

"When the hour fixed for adjournment comes, I will adjourn the meeting, not before."

All the speakers were drowned out except Lucy Stone. This was one of those remarkable occasions when an audience out of control quieted as soon as she began to talk, fascinated by her magnetic qualities which no other speaker possessed. It was said of Lucy's voice that its timbre and pitch were unforgettable. Even after a great lapse of time strangers in a crowd could often identify, her by the sound of it although they could not see her face.

FIVE

Eight years had come and gone now since she left Oberlin. She was thirty-five. All that time she had not wavered in her conviction that marriage was out of the question for a woman who desired as much freedom as she did. It took resolution to remain single, for Lucy was a person of great charm and magnetism, and the men who sought her were of high caliber. She had already, without knowing it, encountered the one she was to marry.

Some time back, while stopping in Cincinnati, she had gone to a hardware dealer to cash a check sent her by the Anti-Slavery Society. Lucy had just undergone a difficult ordeal, having come West to nurse a dying brother. She fell ill herself, and was barely recovered and on her way home.

The young owner of the business, Henry B. Blackwell, waited on her. Their brief transaction over, "something beautiful in her expression" shining through her fatigue, remained with Henry. It was one of those triumphs over appearances which Lucy achieved effortlessly through life.

She had taken her check to the Blackwells, no doubt because she knew the family by reputation, through their abolition sympathies and acquaintance with Garrison. Moreover Henry's sister, Elizabeth Blackwell, who had become the first woman doctor in the country, was as much a target for public persecution as Antoinette Brown.

Henry was seven years younger than Lucy. Like others in his family, he was a fearless advocate of dangerous causes. He was something of a poet and an able writer, besides being a successful speaker and an astute man of business. His liking for people and his sparkling humor had earned him a host of friends.

That first glimpse of Lucy in Cincinnati was never forgotten. Henry later went to two of her lectures; watched her win the rapt interest of her audience, and hold it so for an hour, himself motionless and absorbed. Her secret was unselfconscious, passionate sincerity. After that nothing shook his determination, not even Garrison's insistence that she had already discouraged a number of men. He went to the farm at Coy's Hill armed with a letter from Garrison, and with unconcealed ardor in his blue eyes.

Lucy was standing on the kitchen table when he arrived, her head done up in a towel, a large brush in her hand and a pail of whitewash at her feet. The kitchen ceiling was only half done. She eyed him from her vantage point a trifle suspiciously, but her smile was as disarming as usual. Would he care to wait? She would be through in a few minutes. He had all the time in the world, Henry replied affably, and settled himself in the rocker by the stove with the air of a man who has come to stay.

They went for a long walk afterwards, following the cow path she loved. It was a proper place, on top of Coy's Hill, with the great green arc of the world spread at their feet, for Lucy to explain the high goals she was never going to abandon. After which, it was Henry's turn to enlarge on a theme of his own, the greater goals two might reach together. She listened politely but without a perceptible flicker of emotion.

It took Henry two years of patient arguing and one sensational feat to break through her defenses. His rescue of a Negro child from a Southern slaveholder, who was attempting to take her through the state of Pennsylvania where slavery was unlawful, was a bold stroke which Lucy was quick to applaud. According to law, a slave brought voluntarily by his owners into a free state automatically became free. Henry had boarded the train on which the little girl and her master were traveling, as it drew into the Allegheny City station. Fending off the Southerner's angry resistance, he enabled others to pass the child out to a waiting group of antislavery workers.

For months afterwards he was trailed by slaveholders who threatened to lynch him if they ever caught him on the other side of the Ohio River, and at a mass meeting in Memphis, Tennessee, ten thousand dollars was offered for his head. In spite of his act being upheld by Pennsylvania law, hostility even in free Cincinnati was great enough to damage his business.

It was not only Henry's courage which won Lucy's respect; his clever reversals of her arguments against marriage were unanswerable.

"You ask me," he wrote, "if the laws placed a man in the same situation as they do women, would

I marry? I certainly would. I should first satisfy
myself that you would not be likely to lock me up,
I should require you to promise not to avail yourself
of any unjust laws giving you control of more than
half my future earnings, I should place beyond
your control all my present property. If the marriage were harmonious, the laws would not exist
as far as we were concerned, if it proved discordant
and you should lock me up, I should let myself out
by habeas corpus, and sue you for assault and bat-
tery. I should steal at least half my children from
you and put you to the trouble and expense of a
law suit to get them back—in short, I should be my
own master—

"Why then are women so terribly oppressed,
you may say? Because they have not as a class the
education, the spirit, the energy, the disposition to
be free. Give me a free man, he can never be a
slave. Give me a free woman, she can never be made
one either."

When a speaking tour brought Lucy near Henry's section
of the country, she was persuaded to stay in the Blackwell
home while he attended to the business of advertising her
meetings and engaging the halls. As he had hoped, deep
affection developed between his mother and her young guest.
Intimacy grew and thrived so gradually by this maneuver,
that it finally seemed to Lucy the most natural thing in the
world to marry Henry.

She would have liked to have had Antoinette officiate at

her wedding, but the latter had been ordained in another state, and could not, for that reason, marry anyone in Massachusetts. Thomas Wentworth Higginson, widely known for his courageous, liberal views, performed the ceremony in the small, low-ceilinged farm house at Coy's Hill, on the first day of May, 1855. Lucy was thirty-seven and she had never looked more charming. A cheerful fire on the old hearth threw warm lights on the bride's dress of old-rose silk and on the sprig of orange blossoms in her hair. The Bloomer costume, worn with both valor and discomfort, had been discarded a year ago.

Hand in hand, before their wedding guests, the pair opened the ceremony by reading aloud their "protest" against the inequalities of marital law, written and signed by them both. The text was published next day in the Worcester *Spy*. It began with this statement:

> "While we acknowledge our mutual affection by publicly assuming the relation of man and wife, yet in justice to ourselves and a great principle, we deem it a duty to declare that this act on our part implies no sanction of, nor promise of voluntary obedience to, such of the present laws of marriage as refuse to recognize the wife as an independent, rational being, while they confer upon the husband an injurious and unnatural superiority, investing him with legal powers which no honorable man would exercise, and which no man should possess. We protest especially against the laws which give to the husband:

"1. The custody of the wife's person.

"2. The exclusive control and guardianship of their children.

"3. The sole ownership of her personal and use of her real estate, unless previously settled upon her, or placed in the hands of trustees, as in the case of minors, lunatics and idiots.

"4. The absolute right to the product of her industry."

The declaration wound up with the listing of several other injustices, and then the marriage ritual, omitting certain terms like *obey*, but fulfilling all legal requirements, was performed.

They were both fully prepared for the reception their "Protest" received as soon as it was issued. Whoever attacked the marriage laws laid himself open to scandalous rumor. It was sincerely believed by many now that Henry Blackwell and Lucy Stone were not lawfully wedded. The reputation of one as an unblushing female champion of woman's rights, and of the other as a fanatic who snatched their rightful property from slave owners, was sufficient evidence.

Lucy was too well known to escape being caricatured in popular ditties. One, in which a masterful male was invoked to put a stop to her crusading, ended with this apostrophe:

> *A name like Curtius' shall be his*
> *On fame's loud trumpet blown*
> *Who with a wedding kiss shuts up*
> *The mouth of Lucy Stone!*

Masculine disgust was general when, instead of silencing the lady, Henry defied the ridicule of his own sex to aid a good cause.

People would soon have forgotten the "Protest," if Lucy had not driven its meaning home with a refusal to be called Mrs. Henry Blackwell. Realizing what would be said of her remaining Lucy Stone after marriage, she had fortified her position with the best legal advice. There was no actual law, she was assured, requiring a woman to drop her own name in favor of her husband's. It was merely a custom.

Many of Lucy's best friends thought she was making a great to-do over an unimportant matter. As the Bloomer costume revolt struck the first blow for freedom in dress, so her present stand blazed a new trail. Susan and Elizabeth hailed it as a brave defense of individuality, and Henry, believing that women must develop the "disposition to be free," firmly supported her.

A vital principle lay behind all Lucy's defiance of conventions. Twenty-eight years after her death, her lone crusade had gained enough supporters for the formation of a Lucy Stone League, and today professional women who marry retain their own names as a matter of course. The right to work and achieve and to be identified with what they do is no longer questioned.

SIX

Henry's financial prospects immediately after marriage were still suffering as a result of his rescue of the slave child in Allegheny City. Pending a change in his business and the establishment of their separate home, he and Lucy went back to the house he had bought for his mother in Ohio. There Lucy went on with her lecturing for women and for abolition, and there she became involved in one of the most lurid of the tragedies connected with the Underground Railroad.

A fugitive slave had smuggled his wife and children into the state. There the family was caught before the Underground could help. Ohio was one of those border territories where the poor wretches who failed in their dash for freedom were never given fair trial.

As the chase closed in on them, the young wife, a beautiful mulatto, would have done away with all four of her children had there been time. She was desperately determined to spare her little girl the horrors suffered by women slaves. This one child she managed to kill swiftly, almost decapitating it with one stroke of her knife.

The case stirred so much excitement in Cincinnati that a

hundred armed sheriffs surrounded the jail and courthouse. Against such a force antislavery sympathizers were powerless, but Lucy visited the prisoners and her conversation with the Negro mother was overheard.

At the trial next day, she was asked if it were true that she had offered the woman a knife. Her answer, scornful and distinct, rang in the tense silence of the courtroom like a judgment.

"I did ask her if she had a knife," she replied quietly. "If I were a slave as she is a slave, with the law against me, and society against me, and the church against me, and with no other death-dealing weapon at hand, I would with my own teeth tear open my veins, and send my soul back to God who gave it."

Stricken momentarily with guilt, the slaveholder assured Lucy that he would free Margaret, the wife, but he lied. She was sent manacled down the Ohio River by boat, at night. Months afterwards Lucy heard from the husband. During the journey the boat listed heavily at one point, and Margaret's baby rolled off her lap into the water. She let it go without making a move to save it. Still later, the flat-bottomed craft was wrecked and everyone thrown into the river. Margaret went down, fighting off rescue. Mrs. Stone would be glad to know, he felt sure, that his wife had found freedom at last.

SEVEN

Not long after this incident the Blackwells moved East and bought a modest property in New Jersey. It was Lucy's first home. Here a little girl was born, and the question arose whose name she should bear. Henry reasoned that since Lucy had had all the trouble of bringing her into the world, she should be Alice Stone, but Lucy, with whom the decision was left, called her Alice Stone Blackwell, after them both.

While their child was small, the Blackwells dropped active crusading. A slight injury to Alice while Lucy was absent for a day caused the decision; Henry, during the next eleven years, had to build up a business, and at this period the Civil War put a virtual stop to all other activities. Although motherhood and war interrupted the old life of campaigning, Lucy's burning convictions kindled interest and drew followers in whatever community she lived.

Because of her early, singlehanded pioneering in the Middle West she was probably the most widely known suffrage leader in the country.

The New Jersey State Suffrage Association came into being during her residence in the state. She spoke eloquently, though in vain, before the New Jersey legislature to plead revival of an old state law, originally sponsored by the Quakers, by which Negroes and women property owners had once been empowered to vote. This failing, she staged, during one of Henry's absences on business, a typically Yankee rebellion.

The New Jersey home was in her name. Letting the taxes lapse, she allowed local authorities to seize her household effects and sell them at auction. Little Alice's cradle, autographed pictures of people in public life, tables, chairs and china piled up on the road in front of her house caused quite a commotion in the town. A friendly neighbor, hearing of the sale, bought back most of her furniture. In the meantime, the news spread everywhere that Lucy Stone had resisted "taxation without representation."

At the close of the Civil War, she and Henry plunged immediately into the stormy struggle to enfranchise Negroes and women by one and the same enactment. The attempt grew into a conflict. Public opinion favored giving the ballot to the liberated slave but violently opposed woman suffrage. The sex issue so endangered the Negro's chances that abolitionists, who had long supported women's rights, asked them to withdraw their claims at this time.

It was a great deal to ask of a group which saw its own freedoms slipping out of reach with the passage of every new law. Only two years before, woman suffrage received a setback in the passage of a Fourteenth Amendment to the Constitution which established all voting citizens as "male." The Fifteenth Amendment, now proposed by Abolitionists, provided that no one should be denied the vote "on account of race, color or previous condition of servitude." The insertion of the three-letter word *sex* in the clause would have accomplished all that women wanted. It was to take fifty more years to write it in.

EIGHT

Under stress of watching their own cause defeated, or, at best, delayed for generations, the three friends, Elizabeth Cady Stanton, Susan B. Anthony and Lucy fell into sharp disagreement. Henry and Lucy labored unceasingly to have the word *sex* added to the Fifteenth Amendment, until it became plain that this would kill the measure, and with it Negro suffrage.

Long ago, when there had seemed to be no one else to fight for women, Lucy had let the better-supported antislavery cause take second place. Faced again with the same choice, her heart revolted. Of the three suffrage leaders she had been closest to a debasing system. She had seen the recapture of fugitive slaves and tasted their despair. One more door was opening for the Negro. Should he be compelled to wait until it admitted women? She let it be known that she would not "lift a finger" to hinder his enfranchisement. Her stand disappointed Elizabeth and Susan and the rift between them, which had begun when Elizabeth and Susan affiliated the Cause with persons of doubtful reputation, widened.

The first of these had been George Francis Train. The

second was the notorious clairvoyant Victoria Woodhull, whose brilliant campaigning for woman's rights overshadowed all else in the eyes of Elizabeth and Susan, including the fact that she practiced free love as openly as she preached it.

Mrs. Woodhull's activities were headline gossip. Her brief but glittering career as a suffragist gave newspaper reporters a field day, and did nothing to refute the old accusation that woman's rights encouraged loose morals. Susan woke up before long to the dangers of allowing extremists into her ranks, but not before this particularly flagrant episode had damaged the Movement.

One after another, differences of policy between the leading suffragists in New York and the Blackwells' large following in New England and the Middle West increased, until a break was inevitable. Without giving public notice of the intended separation, Elizabeth and Susan now organized a new association under the title *National* Woman Suffrage Association. In addition, they sent out resolutions passed by them, on controversial questions, as though they were the majority, or representative organization.

In view of the fact that the New England group and their adherents were actually more numerous, their action seemed characteristically highhanded and impulsive to Garrison, Phillips and the Blackwells. The latter had no alternative now but to band themselves into what they called the *American* Woman Suffrage Association.

Regardless of the cleavage in the organization, a growing number of eminent thinkers were by now supporting the idea of woman's rights. Crusaders still paid the price of persecution and ridicule, but they at least found themselves in distinguished company. And so it was, that when Lucy and Henry were urged to move back to New England to strengthen the Movement in Massachusetts, they sold their New Jersey home and went to Boston with keen anticipation. Alice was growing into girlhood by this time and Henry's income made it possible to plunge again into their old, never really abandoned vocation as agitators.

NINE

One of the Blackwells' first considerations now was to found a truly representative paper for the woman suffrage movement. Elizabeth and Susan in their weekly, *The Revolution*, launched with money George Francis Train had advanced in a moment of enthusiasm for the feminist cause, were waging more gallant than judicious warfare for numerous unrelated causes; some of which were listed in their issue of July 2, 1868, as follows:

"Educated suffrage, irrespective of sex or color, equal pay for equal work, eight hours labor, abolition of standing armies and party despotisms. Down with the Politicians—UP with the People!"

Frankly incendiary, as its title implied, and loaded with what the New York *Times* sardonically referred to as "literary nitroglycerine," *The Revolution* did not pretend to speak for anyone but its two militant editors.

However, an official mouthpiece was greatly needed at this point, which would neither shock nor alienate public sympathy and which would present a consistently dispassionate, persuasive argument for woman suffrage and woman's rights. To Lucy, who now felt it her task to create such a paper, dramatics were better left out of its columns and title. She named it simply *The Woman's Journal.*

Henry Blackwell launched the enterprise with a donation of a thousand dollars, and Lucy by her own efforts raised approximately nine thousand more. Mary A. Livermore, popular as a lecturer and with a notable record for Civil War nursing, was engaged as the first editor. Later, however, when it was found impossible to retain a paid staff, she was forced to resign.

The Woman's Journal, like most papers dedicated to reform, was a financial dead weight. Only two such tireless and consecrated crusaders as Lucy and Henry would have dreamed of saddling themselves with it. Its function, however, was too vital to be abandoned. They assumed the whole burden of editorship and management until they died, with such help as their daughter was later able to give them. The labor was unrelenting. Lucy often likened the *Journal* to a big baby, having to be fed constantly, and never growing up.

Pounding the pavements of Boston for reluctant advertisers who would keep the paper financially afloat was exhausting work, very different from the old exciting challenge of facing and disarming a hostile audience. But Lucy had never done anything with a flourish. Years of slow, sustained effort had gone into her struggle for an education. Waiting had given her faith deep roots which did not fail her in arid periods. She understood the gradual process of growth. With the patience of an educator she proposed to establish woman suffrage state by state, until enough territory was won to insure passage of a federal amendment. Even Susan came round to the idea when she realized the franchise would never be gained by assault.

The Revolution came to the end of its brilliant but stormy career in less than three years. *The Woman's Journal,* later published as *The Woman Citizen,* outlasted the suffrage organization. Under Lucy's direction it became the rallying center and headquarters for suffrage forces all over the country as well as the voice of the movement. It had many prominent and able contributors. Its aim, as Julia Ward Howe declared in an article in the first issue, was to war not "against men, but as against all that is pernicious to men and women." No doubt Henry and Lucy largely influenced this aim. It upheld the spirit and purpose of their marriage protest, which emphasized partnership in the marriage relation and equal consideration for both sexes.

TEN

It remained for Alice Stone Blackwell, heir of this unifying policy, to heal the breach in the movement. As a child she had been indifferent, had even felt aversion to the cause which so engrossed her parents. Then, when she was twelve, she came upon an article in a magazine which ridiculed the very principles of equality she took for granted. From that moment she was as embattled a young feminist as any crusading parents could have wished for.

Alice's privileged, happy childhood was in sharp contrast to her mother's. For the first time in her life, Lucy began to enjoy long evenings of leisure with her family, while Henry, who was a superb reader, opened up his stores of poetry and literature for Alice. The high-spirited gaiety of father and daughter were not easy for her to share. Sitting quietly apart, her hands busy with household mending, Lucy was wistfully conscious of all her toil-ridden youth had missed.

"In Heaven," she used to console herself smiling, "I may understand music and jokes."

She seemed to forget the feats of scholarship she had achieved. Her vow to learn Greek and Hebrew had been kept,

to the frequent discomfiture of clergymen who tried to con-
found her with scriptural passages whose original meaning
she knew better than themselves. Nor was she ever conscious
of her own genius, the mingled fire and poetry, the persuasive
charm which captivated foe and friend alike.

But Lucy saw to it that Alice acquired breadth of interests
and varied contacts that she herself had never had time for.
When the National Woman Suffrage Association and the
American agreed to bury an old quarrel, it was because
Alice Stone Blackwell, able as a mediator, broad in outlook,
saw the desirability of the reconciliation.

Twenty years had by now modified Susan's militancy. A
younger generation, starting from the vantage won by their
predecessors, was evolving new methods of attack. At the
convention of 1890 which resulted in the merging of the two
factions, the handwriting on the wall was clear. The pioneer
phase of the woman's crusade was over; the day of single
champions had passed; the hour of concerted action had
struck.

Lucy was seventy-one at the time. She could look back on
a life of immense rewards as well as of conflict. The personal
happiness she did not seek, destiny would not let her escape;
for her marriage became, as Henry had predicted it would,
her unique contribution to woman's rights. It was too successful to be a weapon in the hands of ill-wishers. The peace
and affection of her home life, with its comfort and well-being,
painted a picture of domestic content which all the carica-
tures of unsexed Amazons could not efface.

Although the most dramatic events of Lucy's life occurred
during the violent, troubled era before the Civil War, she

and Henry had unforgettable experiences out West, after their return to Massachusetts and active suffrage work. Campaigning in wilderness territory at a time of life when most people seek comfort and ease, they cheerfully "ate all kinds of food, slept in every sort of bed, were bitten by every variety of insect, faced all weathers," as their daughter put it, with the old fortitude of earlier years. Aftereffects from fording a flooded river on one of these later trips brought on rheumatism from which Lucy never entirely recovered. Her crusading was confined to districts near home from then on.

In New England there no longer existed the same violent opposition to women speakers, although there was still enough spite emanating from the pulpit to amuse an aging soldier and keep her in fighting trim.

"I am requested to say," one minister announced a talk by Lucy Stone in his suavest manner, "that a hen will undertake to crow like a cock at the town hall this afternoon at five o'clock. Anybody who wants to hear that kind of music will, of course, attend."

This sort of advertisement had the desired effect of crowding the hall, and the "hen," small, elderly and sweet-faced in lace cap and kerchief, enchanted all who came. Equal rights in this disarming guise captured the house.

As the pace of life slackened, Lucy's memory had time to dwell lovingly on a farm child, climbing a dark and narrow cow path under the stars toward the fiery ladder of dawn.

"I have had a pile of good out of the clouds," she used to say, watching their glory now from the windows of her room.

Her way had led upwards ever since; out from the limitations of her birth to the free heights on which she came to stand. She knew with serenity when the time arrived for her to walk that path again; when labors were finished and earth ties slipped easily from her grasp. Ahead waited freedoms more shining than any she had battled for on earth. She faced the solitary journey as fearlessly as the child Lucy had of old, turning back only for a brief last message to the daughter who would carry on the work she had begun.

"Make the world better," she whispered to Alice before she passed into the shadows, unfrightened, self-reliant and alone.

IV

Susan B. Anthony

"In ancient Greece she would have been a Stoic; in the era of the Reformation, a Calvinist; in King Charles's time a Puritan; but in the Nineteenth Century, by the very laws of her being she is a reformer."

Elizabeth Cady Stanton on Susan B. Anthony

"A lady whose husband had been unsuccessful in business, established herself as a milliner in Manchester. After some years of toil, she realized sufficient for the family to live upon in comfort, the husband having done nothing meanwhile. They lived in easy circumstances, after she gave up business, and then the husband died, bequeathing all his wife's earnings to his own illegitimate children."

Westminster Review, October, 1856

ONE

"The spooler at the mill has fallen suddenly ill. There seems no one to take her place." Here Daniel Anthony paused and glanced at the row of young faces around his supper table as though waiting some comment.

Guelma, Susan and Hannah, whose two years apart made their neat, pigtailed heads look like evenly spaced steps, paused in their eating, too, and fixed questioning eyes on the speaker. It was not like father, who was usually very definite about what to do next, to hesitate.

Nor was it Susan's way. "Why, I can take Jenny's place. I've watched her work and know just what she does. Oh, Father, please let me try. I would so love to earn!" She was out of her chair in her eagerness, her face flushed.

Ignoring the clear disapproval in his wife's eyes, Daniel glanced quizzically at his twelve-year-old daughter. The lift of Susan's chin was almost as stubborn as his own. The patrician cast to her features, the wide forehead and finely arched brows, and the air of sturdy self-reliance were all distinctly Anthony traits. But her smile, glowing and affectionate, was her mother's. It lighted her stern young face with beauty.

It had occurred to Daniel, he had later to admit to his wife, that Susan might jump at the chance he presented to do something that would test her skill and endurance. Of the children she was the quickest and ablest at home tasks and the most ambitious to learn. Had she not mastered long division all by herself, spending long industrious evenings by the kitchen lamp with her figuring, because the local schoolmaster refused to teach an unnecessary amount of arithmetic to girls?

Daniel understood her urge to push on. It had driven him out of farming in the Berkshire hills and into starting a cotton mill; and that, in turn, had led to this bigger enterprise in Battenville, New York, where he was now well established.

"But I've watched Jenny nearly as often as Susan has, and I'd like to earn too. It's only fair to take turns!" Hannah's childish outcry to do everything that Susan did broke into his reflections.

"Now, I am glad thee is ambitious too, but teasing will get thee nowhere," Daniel hushed her firmly. "One pair of inexperienced hands in the factory is all I can allow. However, we'll decide the question fairly." He went to the fireplace and, plucking two straws from the hearth broom, held up their ends. "Come, Hannah, thee may have first draw. Whoever gets the long straw shall do Jenny's work, but she must agree to divide her wages with the loser."

Whether justice really settled the matter or Daniel's maneuvering, the results satisfied all concerned, especially Susan who drew the long straw and thought hard work for half pay very much the best of the bargain.

Next morning the mill hands were surprised to see their employer's young daughter on the spooler's bench, and when the news got around the townfolk thought it strange that the community's most well-to-do citizen should put his child to work in a mill. But Daniel was an independent man, as everyone where he lived soon found out. He had a Quaker belief that work hurt nobody and that a girl had just as much right to learn a trade as a boy.

He was capable, however, of ignoring other Quaker notions, as when he had chosen a Berkshire girl who belonged to the "world's people" for his bride.

Lucy Read, gifted with a voice of remarkable power and beauty and the temperament of an artist, might in a different environment and day have become a famous singer. She had often quarreled with Daniel, the teasing playmate of her childhood, but he had grown into a handsome, masterful lover, head and shoulders above others in brains and ability, as most of the Anthonys were.

Since matrimony was the only career a properly brought up young woman might consider, Lucy not unnaturally embraced this vocation with the same intensity and ardor she had put into singing, renouncing for her Quaker husband much harmless enjoyment besides her music and her Baptist religion.

But she had been the popular belle of the countryside, and before she married her Quaker she had the spirit to claim her right to one final good time. She was never to forget her last intoxicating dance, whirling from the arms of one partner to another. Her feet, that must never keep time to a fiddle again, simply refused to come to a stop. Leaning against the wall, the picture of bored but patient endurance, her escort Daniel generously conceded she might dance until four in the morning, since she had conceded all else. When the news of this escapade reached the ears of local Friends, Daniel was very nearly "read out of meeting."

The habit of continually suppressing her natural instincts eventually made Lucy Anthony a more rigid Quaker than Daniel. She did not sing again, except at her spinning wheel or to croon her babies to sleep, but she dreamed of escape from the enslavement of her narrow life to some high pasture lot, where her voice and her pent-up emotions could be freed.

Because Lucy Anthony lived in a period when women harnessed themselves willingly and even proudly to gigantic domestic labors, she made no objection when Daniel decided that eleven of his factory hands could board in his home. From then on, Lucy seldom cooked or washed for less than sixteen people. Daniel was actually a considerate husband, besides being wealthier than most of his neighbors. Had he seen a need for it, he would and could have provided adequate help for his wife. He saw no more, however, and no better than other fond husbands of his day, with the result that Lucy's sole assistant was a thirteen-year-old child who did light chores for a few hours after school.

It was not long before a portion of the load fell on the young shoulders of Guelma, Susan and Hannah. A baby had been born to Lucy only a few weeks before Jenny the spooler fell ill. During her confinement the three little girls, the oldest of whom was fourteen, did all the cooking, not only for the large Anthony family and their ever-present factory hands, but they also prepared daily lunch pails for some dozen workmen who were firing bricks for Daniel's new house.

Small wonder Susan imagined factory work for a few pennies a day a glamorous adventure! But by the time her two weeks among the spinning bobbins and clattering looms in the cotton mill were over the little girl had learned something about deadly monotony and frustrated impulse.

Hannah bought herself a coveted bit of finery with her half of the wages Susan earned, but Susan remembered that her mother's eyes had rested wistfully on six bright blue teacups, gayer than any a Quaker's wife should own. Happily, they were still on the store shelf when she hastened there to buy them.

The mill episode was symbolic of Susan's life. It was a pattern of unceasing labor toward a selfless goal which she was to repeat as long as she lived.

On those rare occasions in after years when Susan could be induced to talk about herself, she spoke lovingly of her childhood. Its hardships had, after all, been shared, and the injustices to which it awoke her were, through her own efforts, fast becoming a thing of the past.

(She was, moreover, of that lucky generation of children who had seen homemaking practiced as a primitive art and a co-operative family industry. At six she had been set by the fire to turn the crisply browning meat while it roasted over the hearth. She remembered the succulent hiss of spitting fat and of hot juice from toasting apples, falling into the embers. The big Dutch oven by the fireplace had filled her childhood and her memory with rich, good flavors and odors. How eagerly she had raced home from school on biting winter days, because along with the chores awaiting her in the big kitchen there would be the smell of freshly baked loaves, a taste of fruit simmering in spices, the aroma of herbs in the evening stew, and a piece of hot gingerbread, as big as her fist.

TWO

The Anthonys lived comfortably as did most energetic country-folk in those days, skilled in home crafts and proud of their thrift and industry. If their house stood near traveled roads and their hospitality was generous, they could expect to keep more or less open house, and, since heavy drinking was a generally accepted habit, most cellars were stocked with rum, brandy and gin.

To their discomfiture, guests found no hard liquor on Friend Anthony's bountifully spread table. Neither did he permit smoking in his home. The one exception he made to this rule was for the benefit of Elders and Preachers of the Quaker sect who stopped at the Anthony home on their way to Quarterly meetings. These pious gentlemen had free access to the closet under the stairs, where demijohns, clay pipes and tobacco were stored. While their host did not encourage them to sin, the door was left unlocked!

Quaker prohibitions at that period were often fanatical on matters of no importance. Daniel was reprimanded before a committee several times, once for buying a fine camel's-hair coat with a cape, a warm and needed protection against the cold of his long cross-country drives on business. The coat was declared to be "out-of-plainness"; too costly and therefore too ostentatious for Quaker wear. It was also noted with disapproval that Daniel's wife sang lullabies to her children. But there was no Quaker ban on distilled liquor. Daniel's ideas on the subject were his own and in keeping with the independence he never lost. As he had ignored the Quaker edict against taking a wife from "the world's people," he also ignored the command to give up his warm coat.

While the cause of temperance had only a few isolated adherents, Daniel, whose brains and abilities made him a leader in whatever community he joined, took a courageous stand for it; a fact never forgotten by the young daughter who was to pioneer in an equally unpopular crusade. Tavern keepers who expected increased business from the presence of his factories and mills were his bitterest opponents. Daniel hired no one who was known to be habitually drunk and required a pledge from his workers to stay off anything stronger than cider or wine.

All trade was transacted at that period under the genial influence of a demijohn. So usual was it to negotiate a bargain with rum, that young Daniel's first concern, on leaving the home farm to become a merchant, was to stock up with this commodity. One morning, however, a fellow tradesman in his locality was found lying frozen in the road beside a jug which told its own sordid story. Although he himself had had no part in the tragedy, Daniel made up his mind then and there that he would rather fail in business than exploit another man's weakness.

The test of this decision came soon, when a prosperous cot-

ton merchant in Battenville, New York, offered him a partnership and a chance for much greater expansion. Leaving the
Berkshires behind him for good, Daniel also turned his back
on former business practices.

The day the Anthony family arrived in Battenville with
their household effects and merchandise, Daniel's partner
watched with dismay as bales and boxes were emptied out of
his wagon and carried into the store.

"Why, Anthony," he exclaimed, "where are the rum
barrels?"

"There aren't any."

"You don't expect to keep store without rum, do you? If
you don't treat no one will trade with you."

"Then I'll close the store," retorted Daniel, and he meant
it.

His partner's prophecy was quickly borne out. Customers
entered, and when no drink was proffered, insolently ex-
amined cupboards and even searched the cellar. Finding none
of the desired hospitality, they walked out in disgust. But
business integrity won out in a day when shoddy merchandise
was too easily slipped over the counter along with the rum. No
one got cheated at Friend Anthony's store. The news spread
and he began to outsell his competitors.

Nevertheless, the argument for liquor cropped up at every
turn. In order to build quarters for his mill hands in the new
locality, Daniel staged the usual house-raising.

"No gin? No volunteers," warned his partner again.

"All right then, the houses won't go up," replied Daniel
with exasperating calm.

Instead of gin, the Anthony family offered gallons of

lemonade and the best gingerbread Battenville had ever tasted. Everyone was sober, the buildings went up in record time and there was not a single accident. It was the talk of the town— until another house-raising in the old style obliterated its memory.

There were reasons why working men were always willing to work for Daniel on his own terms. He was a strict and far from easygoing employer, but he was fair. It was known that he hated slavery and refused to buy cotton grown by unpaid labor when other was available. His sense of what industry owed its laborers was far in advance of his time. He not only watched over the moral welfare of his employees but organized a free night school for them, which he taught himself when instructors were lacking.

Doubtless many a country community at that time owed its one good school to some Quaker citizen who had to educate his children according to Quaker standards. Daniel himself, as soon as his means permitted, took his family out of the Battenville district school and started a private one of his own.

Young people were neither pampered nor was idleness encouraged in Susan's girlhood—least of all in Daniel Anthony's household. When Guelma and Susan were each fifteen they taught the summer session for smaller pupils in their father's school. At seventeen, Susan earned her board and keep for a full year, teaching.

The Quaker way of life offered the young few diversions and certainly no frivolities, however innocent. Susan was elated over this first independent adventure away from home with its meagre pay of five dollars a month, while Daniel's neighbors were as shocked as when he put her to work in his factory. Only girls who had no male relative to support them, or whom poverty or other misfortune forced to be wage earners, left the shelter of home to work for hire.

However, it did Battenville no harm to see its wealthiest citizen send his daughters out into the world to develop their full capacities as though they had been sons. It was Daniel's purpose to enrich their minds and widen their experience as far as his means permitted. Unfortunately, however, just as the girls were ready for more education than home schools afforded, the nationwide panic of 1837 began to affect his income. He therefore sent Guelma to a boarding school outside of Philadelphia, which seems to have had little to recommend it save a very moderate tuition.

THREE

Here Susan joined her sister the winter following her year
of apprentice teaching. She was eighteen, and in spite of
great self-reliance she was as naïve as any other country girl
who had never been more than six miles from home. At this
time, too, she was fast becoming a youthful prig. For Susan
had Daniel's drive and her mother's strong emotions, and for
these powerful inheritances her Quaker upbringing had given
her no outlet but duty.

Buried under stern young pedantry was the smile which
had once been so disarming and eager, and twelve months'
dismal piety learned at Miss Deborah Moulson's Academy
for Young Females did nothing to revive it. Not until liberating association with many types of people taught her to throw
off the joyless teachings she received in adolescence, did the
real Susan emerge again, uninhibited, rebellious and free.

Her year in a boarding school, which had been the longed-
for event of her girlhood, proved unhappy. The headmistress,
Deborah Moulson, was one of those grim disciplinarians who
seem fantastic now, but who were entirely too credible and
too numerous in their day.

Because Susan showed the greatest ability of any pupil, Deborah took the most pains with her. This meant that she must be treated with crushing severity lest she lose the virtue of humility. If, for example, she forgot to dot an *i*, the omission was flaunted before the school like a major offense.

Youthful blunders and unintentional accidents were cruelly rebuked. One morning, Susan, trained at home in habits of tidiness, detected a cobweb on the schoolroom ceiling. Her impulse was to remove it and the top of Miss Moulson's desk was just the right height for the maneuver. She climbed up.

The cobweb was obliterated with one flick of her handkerchief, but Susan had not calculated on her sturdy young weight. She heard an ominous snap as she raised her arm. Horrified, she remained there, afraid to move. When she dared get down, the girls crowded round sympathetically.

"Thee need not worry. See, it is only a hinge broken!" A babble of relief rose in the room followed by a sudden rush back to their seats. Deborah Moulson had come in unexpectedly, summoned by the teacher in charge.

"I have broken your desk," said Susan in the awful silence.

But Deborah was not going to let her off easily or quickly through confession. She pretended not to have heard, while she questioned the teacher. How came her desk top to be broken? Who did it? How was it possible for a grown girl to be so thoughtless? Was it not evident that even a child should not step on so fragile a piece? So the inquisition went on, all details of the crime being rehearsed, while Susan stood mortified and ignored. When Miss Moulson was ready to deal personally with her victim, Susan had fled to her room, her heart bursting with humiliation and grief.

Occasional laughter and happy nonsense—all normal young behavior—was exaggerated into wickedness by this fanatical Quaker. One of her unique punishments, when she fancied her students merited extra severity, was to deprive the whole school of recitations. Once the curriculum was interrupted for eleven days because of some imagined offense.

Since no one but Susan had a passion to learn, this penalty amounted to persecution of the one ardent young student whose phenomenal memory and strong, healthy body were perhaps more than a consumptive headmistress could bear. Deborah Moulson was actually dying of tuberculosis.

Susan's diary at this period records anguished bewilderment rather than resentment. The most innocent motives and acts were judged wicked by Miss Moulson. It was all very confusing to a devout little country Quaker, who strove earnestly for perfection and wept bitterly in secret over her failures.

No plaint of injustice appears in her letters home, and for a very good reason. Following the usual custom of headmistresses then, all letters were brought to Deborah for correction before they could be mailed. This method not only forestalled any clandestine correspondence with members of the opposite sex (a major crime in all female institutions), but successfully quashed any murmurs of discontent.

Instead, Susan, like all her schoolmates, perjured her young soul with sugary references to her "dear Teacher" and the "agreeable" school in which she·hoped her younger sisters might also be placed. That the hypocrisy was forced upon her, made it none the less harmful. Even her diary was full of moral platitudes and extravagant piety. Susan was not only imitating her pompous elders, but gorging her starved young affections on religious emotion, the one indulgence that was not forbidden.

The last drop added to her cup of misery during this dreadful year was the nearsightedness which hampered her studies. No one thought of putting spectacles on young people at that period and fear of failure and reprimand made Susan's eye trouble more acute. The scars left by her ordeal at Miss Moulson's lasted for years. They were part of a groundless sense of inferiority which paralyzed her whenever she heard the flow of Elizabeth Cady Stanton's wit and eloquence. Her pen had been "mounted on stilts" in youth, Susan asserted, and had great difficulty in coming down.

FOUR

At the end of that year in boarding school, a long, nation-wide depression following the 1837 financial crash began. Daniel Anthony, along with countless other industrialists, big and little, faced ruin. Susan and Guelma came back to Batten-ville to find the brave mother, whom no task had ever broken, sick with discouragement. Their father had aged. He watched the collapse of his life's effort stoically, but Susan knew he suffered. Her own miseries of the past months—how small they seemed in comparison!

The home they had all helped build with industry and love had to be abandoned. Everything it contained, even the boys' pocketknives and their parents' spectacles, were being confiscated by creditors.

Out of the wreck of Daniel's affairs, there remained a small satinet factory and a gristmill, two or three miles from Battenville. He had managed to cling to these, although they were heavily mortgaged, hoping by their means to gradually rebuild a business.

During the next five years the Anthonys lived near these two enterprises, in a large house that had once been a road tavern. Its second story held an immense dance hall whose flooring, local tradition claimed, was laid over glass bottles to give extra resonance to the music of the fiddlers. This room, unused by the family, became the cause of Daniel's being finally "read out of Quaker meeting."

The young people in the locality asked permission to use it for their weekly dances; their only other alternative, they reminded Daniel, would be to apply to the public tavern, and this they felt sure Friend Anthony would be loath to approve. Dancing was one form of worldly indulgence that had never appealed to Daniel. He had observed the Quaker ban regarding it rigidly. Now, however, it seemed far worse to subject youth to bad influences than to let them dance under his roof.

His neighbors' sons and daughters met therefore weekly in the Anthony home, and as a concession to Lucy Anthony, the girls, Guelma, Susan and Hannah, were allowed to join their friends, provided they accepted no partners. Lucy's heart ached for her three young daughters more than their own did. With hands folded tight in the laps of their plain Quaker frocks, their cheeks and eyes bright and their feet tapping a surreptitious accompaniment to the lilt of the fiddles, they were torn between a longing to join the fun and astonishment at the cavorting of country youth. To the three sedate Quaker maids it was enough dissipation to laugh and chatter with the crowd and share the refreshments their mother always provided.

But the happy sound of jig tunes and square dancing carried farther than Daniel supposed. It eventually reached the ears of the Society of Friends to which he belonged, and for this,

his latest breach of Quaker rule, he was promptly disowned. Elders had been lenient with his several violations until now, because of the prestige his better education and abilities lent their group.

Daniel accepted dismissal with ironic composure. "For one of the best acts of my life, the best religious society in the world has turned me out," he summed up the illogic of Quaker reasoning.

During these years the entire Anthony family joined forces to save what was left of Daniel's business. The oldest boy, now sixteen, went to work in the gristmill, and Daniel himself labored with his mill hands. Guelma was married soon after leaving Miss Moulson's, but Susan and Hannah taught school steadily, summer and winter sessions, and turned over to their father whatever they could spare from their earnings. These loans from his daughters, made at great cost to his pride, Daniel repaid in time.

The knowledge that further schooling had become out of the question was bitter to Susan. The smattering of philosophy and chemistry received at Miss Moulson's had opened up new fields she could never explore unless she found time for laborious self-teaching.

Away from home a great deal of the time now, and living among non-Quakers, Susan began to weigh and sift for herself the influences of her youth. It was a lonely period of puzzled groping in an alien world, but it hastened her maturing. She had her first encounter with race prejudice in a Friends' Meeting House in New Rochelle. There she saw Negroes relegated to the balcony because white Quakers would not sit beside them. Susan was shocked.

This—from her own people who prided themselves on a doctrine of equality!)

And when she wrote home about it, Guelma's husband, Aaron McLean, cautioned her to be "prudent"! Hateful word that all her life would act as a goad. She could hardly wait to write her father what she knew would reach Aaron McLean's ears—that she had called on these despised Christians of a different race and found them cultured and refined, and in many ways superior to some Quakers.

To provincial, Quaker-reared Susan, the metropolitan dailies circulating in New Rochelle revealed astounding facts about the President of her country. During his recent visit to New York City Van Buren had twice attended that iniquitous spectacle, the theater! Here was an example of sin in "high places," as disturbing as her discovery that the nation's leaders partook freely (in her own shocked words) of the "all-debasing wine."

Aaron McLean felt no call to defend theater-going, but he wished to inform a naïve young sister-in-law that drinking was the custom—especially among politicians. At a recent political banquet in Boston not less than twenty-three hundred bottles of champagne had been consumed. And was she aware that the Senator from Kentucky, Henry Clay, of whom she thought so highly, not only drank but owned slaves? A slave body servant, in fact, stood at Clay's elbow in full view of his audiences all the while he made impassioned speeches for liberty! So much for the inconsistency of public men.

When Susan was reliably informed that President Van Buren was respectable, God-fearing and a very moderate drinker, even though he was sadly in need of salvation on the subject of playgoing, she had to alter her opinion again. But though her inner conflict was deep and perplexing, she was at least free to do her own thinking. Unwillingly, yet with an inherent honesty which the pious humbug taught her in adolescence no longer choked, she began to reshuffle her values.

Injustices that she had never been conscious of before became obvious and galling as she continued to teach. District schools had several times engaged her, after a male teacher had failed either to discipline or teach satisfactorily. In each case Susan did a better job than her predecessor and received exactly one-quarter of his pay.

There was also the matter of her mother's inheritance, which all these years had been in the safekeeping of an uncle, because married women were permitted no legal control over their own property.

When at the end of five years of persistent bad times, Daniel found himself forced to abandon his remaining factory and mill, this untouched fund left by Grandfather Read to his daughter provided the down payment on a farm in Rochester to which Daniel moved the family.

But what would have happened to them all if Uncle Joshua Read had spent the sum entrusted to him for his own needs? Many a man upon whom helpless women relatives, who had no power to sue a dishonest guardian or trustee, depended had not resisted so easy a temptation. The girl Susan must have been aware of this family situation and had doubtless heard of women less fortunate than her mother.

Growing knowledge and disillusionment with the very average men she met in girlhood, made her cling more stubbornly to the high standards her father had set. It is quite probable that Susan never found anyone she cared deeply enough to marry. During youth she was never to lack suitors. Since it took a hardy woman to survive the continual child-bearing and care of the immense households of those days, there were always some widowers looking for exactly the strong, young, and capable second wife Susan would have made.

These discomfited gentlemen are referred to casually in her letters as escorts, never as lovers. Delicacy closed her lips on the subject all her life, for Susan was not only an incurable idealist; she was secretly romantic. By the time she was moving in a bigger world and meeting men of her own caliber, she was completely dedicated to a life of public service.

FIVE

The farm in Rochester, to which the Anthonys moved, would, it was hoped, provide a living for them all as well as a roof. The family was much smaller since both Guelma and Hannah had married and young Daniel had found work in Massachusetts. Of the children there remained only Susan, now twenty-five, eighteen-year-old Mary, and Merritt, a boy of eleven.

The thinly settled country close to Lake Ontario looked very bleak to the five, when, after a seven-days' journey by stage and canal boat, they landed at the foot of Fitzhugh street in Rochester, on a damp afternoon in November. Daniel had only ten dollars left in his pocket. Lodgings for the night were out of the question. There was nothing for it but to hitch up the horse and wagon they had brought with them and try to reach their farm before dark.

Lucy Anthony had never needed more courage than on that slow, bitterly cold drive to a home she had never seen, that she could only pray would be less dismal than the surrounding countryside. Susan fought her own dejection by encouraging· chatter with the small brother, huddled for warmth between herself and Mary on the back seat. Old friends had made adversity bearable at home; this was a harsher kind, to be faced alone and unfriended.

The wagon swayed and bumped over the rutted road jostling its occupants unmercifully. Daniel threw a protective arm around his wife and Susan saw their eyes meet in a long, comforting look.

"They don't mind where they go. They are together," she thought, a sudden lump in her throat.

Night came before they reached the farm. Faint light from a kitchen window guided them into the drive and the door was opened by an old man left there to mind the livestock till the new owners arrived. Cramped and stiff from their chill drive, the travelers groped their way into the dimly lit house, too glad to have reached shelter to care what sort it was.

Daniel had bought no food in Rochester, expecting to repay the caretaker for the simple supper most farmers could provide. It proved simpler than they had imagined. He had nothing in the house but cornmeal, the aged native informed them, and the evening's milk, indicating the pail he had brought in.

But an hour later a grateful odor of warmth and nourishment rose from Lucy's kettle of steaming hot mush, beaten to a light yellow froth with her wooden spoon. Daniel, coming in out of the raw night after inspecting his barns and the small farm smithy where he was going to tinker and forge to his heart's content, declared he had never tasted better. There was a note of eager confidence in his voice that had not been there for some months.

Sensing the change in him, Susan felt a load lifted. She saw how a man could be reborn by a return to living growth and to skills learned in boyhood. The wide boards of the oak floor, on which she and Mary and young Merritt had to spend the night because there was only one bed in the house, felt much less hard because of that knowledge.

New environment and new associations did even more for Daniel. In a few months he was successfully involved in business again, this time with the New York Life Insurance Company, just starting in Rochester. After that, the farm which had provided a needed breathing space between two periods in his career became a hobby as well as a home.

SIX

Susan remained with her parents for about six months, her tireless enthusiasm for work a help to them both in getting settled. But like Daniel her talents were bound to draw her out of obscurity and into greater usefulness. A letter arrived shortly from the Canajoharie Academy in New York. It was signed by Uncle Joshua Read and two other school trustees and it offered her entire charge of the "female department."

This was a position of greater responsibility than Susan had ever filled and with a larger salary. Other inducements were the prospect of staying with Uncle Joshua's daughters who lived close to the school. Canajoharie was, besides, only seventy-five miles or so from Battenville and Easton, where Guelma and Hannah were settled.

Susan set out with some qualms as to her fitness for the new work and apparently none at being plunged into a more worldly life with her mother's non-Quaker relatives. Since Daniel's dismissal from his Society of Friends the Anthonys still attended Quaker meetings, but no longer felt bound by its disciplines.

In the interval, experience had broadened Susan and modified many of her puritanical opinions but not her abhorrence of the liquor evil. She was too much Daniel's daughter not to have inherited his diehard principles. With such a father, too, she may have been better informed than most girls on the effects of alcoholism. That innocent women and children were its chief victims she could have seen without going far to look, at a period when confirmed drunkenness was not grounds for divorce, and conventions forced women to bear the unwanted and often sickly children of a degraded father.

While much too levelheaded to be trapped by vanity and her own emotions, Susan dreamed and thought about marriage as much as any girl, and the next three years spent among cousins who encouraged harmless frivolities and amusements were to offer her every chance to meet men and form the longed-for "attachment." While with her mother's relatives, she not only lost the Quaker habit of speech but threw off many of the prohibitions that she now realized were senseless.

All the youth she had missed seems to have been crowded into this brief gay period.

No part of her salary needing to be sent home now, she spent most of it on clothes she had never hoped to own or been able to afford. What vicarious enjoyment Lucy Anthony must have derived from Susan's accounts of her purchases, can be imagined. They were described in detail for her, from "blue prunella gaiters" to the modish "puffs" on a new muslin gown and the "pearl straw gypsy hat," beflowered and beribboned contrary to all Quaker rules.

At the Canajoharie Academy she became the adored young mistress whose admirers plunged her students in flutters of excitement. Her pupils outdid the others at school exercises. In her elegant plaid, made specially for such occasions, and with her chestnut braids piled high in the latest coronet fashion, the new teacher looked a veritable queen, as the rapt gaze of certain interested parties testified. Townsfolk who had disapproved engaging an attractive young mistress remarked that it was just as they had foreseen. The "female department" would soon be minus a teacher again.

The success of her pupils at these school functions gave Susan all the palpitations of a prima donna. Applause on top of so much nervous tension was a little intoxicating, and added the sparkle needed to give her beauty. On summer vacations with Guelma and Hannah she showed off her finery and flaunted her freedom before her sisters already burdened with family cares. Spinsterhood, so humiliating to women of her generation, had decided advantages, she found. The small triumph amused her, brief though it was.

For in her third year at Canajoharie much that had been novel began to pall on poor Susan. She saw nothing romantic about being escorted home at the end of an evening by a half-tipsy gallant, and began to refuse to go to dances unless she could have "a total abstinence man," a fairly impossible requirement.

Her work as headmistress ceased to be a challenge, now she had already proved herself. She had reached the highest goal a woman teacher could attain in those days. On top of growing boredom, Susan was depressed by the tragedy unfolding in the home in which she lived.

The cousin Margaret, with whom she boarded, had been failing steadily following the birth of her fourth child. She was closer than a sister to Susan. It was Margaret who had known just what was needed to soften and heighten Susan's good looks. It was she who had encouraged delightful extravagances, like the gray fox muff and a coveted gold brooch. Who but Margaret had taken such pride in her successes? In whom else could she confide so easily?

Susan nursed her cousin devotedly every minute she could spare from school, but she had to stand silently by, watching strength and life ebb, while a self-centered husband minimized his wife's real ills and magnified every little headache of his own. Margaret died, leaving Susan heartsick, and with some new and bitter conclusions about marriage.

At the close of school a few months later, Susan left Canajoharie for good. She wanted a vacation from teaching and needed to get away from a locality spoiled for her by unhappy associations. Stopping for a last brief visit with her sisters, she went back to Rochester.

SEVEN

It was a homecoming in more than one sense. Susan had had her fling. She had walked in those meadows which had looked from behind Quaker barriers, so green and smooth, so flowered with pleasures; and she had found them deceiving, sown with coarser grass than she had supposed and pitted with holes. The lesson burned deeper than if she had been able to learn it gradually, through a lighthearted youth.

At home she found Daniel's insurance business well established, the farm in need of good management and her mother somewhat broken in health. Following the family tradition, Mary was teaching while Merritt had already left home.

Insisting that her mother needed to rest, Susan took over most of the housework, finding relief in it from the unsettling emotions, the distaste with old interests, and the temporary bewilderment which seemed the aftermath of her recent experiences. Through her healthy veins ran a tireless flow of energy. How use it? For the first time the sense of a larger destiny tugged at her imagination.

And while the feeling remained like an insistent call, she plunged into occupations the land offered. The peach trees

Daniel had planted had come into full bearing and a large crop was going to waste because he lacked time now to manage the place. Susan went out with the workers to oversee the plowing, planting and picking. She farmed with intelligence, enthusiasm and energy.

But it could not satisfy her perpetual hunger of intellect. Fortunately she had come home just in time to take part in heated debates over slavery, temperance and woman's rights—three burning questions then agitating Rochester. Moreover, her father's house had become in her absence the gathering place for all independent, liberal thinkers in town.

Antislavery sentiment was growing. In Rochester the Underground Railway operated with the tacit knowledge of most of its citizens. Although the subject was never mentioned, many knew what families were taking in escaped slaves and smuggling them over the Canadian border. Added to this hidden drama was a visible one, the arrival in Rochester of the Negro, Frederick Douglass, one of the most picturesque of the great abolition figures. It was in Rochester that Douglass launched his abolition paper, *The North Star*. One of Daniel's first acts, on Susan's return from Canajoharie, was to take her to call on Douglass, already his close friend.

This connection with the antislavery cause drew other distinguished crusaders to the Anthony home. Sunday evenings, when as many as twenty able thinkers sat around the long supper table, to share their ardent convictions or discuss the South's latest threat of secession, were to remain the most glowing memories of Susan's youth. Garrison, Wendell Phillips, Channing, Douglass and other abolitionists who visited Rochester were often of the party. Absorbed in the talk, yet proud of her skill as a cook, Susan made agonized attempts to be in the kitchen without missing what was being said in the dining room.

Another issue which engrossed her, and in which she had been very prominent in Canajoharie, was the cause of temperance. Soon after coming home again she had sought membership in the Rochester chapter of women temperance workers. The Daughters of Temperance were a timid, ineffectual band, whose main function was to applaud the decisions of the Brothers of Temperance. Susan, however, had yet to discover this fact.

Out of these two reforms, and largely because of them, a third cause was slowly emerging. A year back, in 1848, while she was still teaching in Canajoharie, she had heard of the birth of a Woman's Rights Movement in Seneca Falls. The convention there had adjourned, to meet a few days later in Rochester. Susan's mother and her sister Mary had both been interested spectators of the Rochester meeting, and had given her vivid accounts of its prime instigators, Lucretia Mott and Elizabeth Cady Stanton.

Susan was curious and eager about the new subject, but unconvinced that the franchise was a need. She had been brought up among people who never voted anyway, for Quakers neither sanctioned nor supported governments that resorted to war.

She was teaching briefly now, whenever she was asked to fill in a vacancy, but the monotony of the schoolroom had become unbearable. She had caught a fervor for causes from the men and women who frequented her father's house, in whose eyes burned a fanatic devotion. It was a fiery contagion, but as yet it gave her no guide to her special mission. For a while she plunged into temperance work, organizing small branch societies for women.

During this time, Abby Kelley and her husband, Stephen Foster, arrived in Rochester to speak against slavery. To Susan their coming was an event. Abby had been among the very earliest women abolition speakers, a fellow martyr with Angelina and Sarah Grimké and Lucretia Mott. Humbly, yet unmistakably, Susan was beginning to recognize her affinity with women of this stamp. She went with the Fosters when they left Rochester on a week's speaking tour. It was her initiation into the hardships of crusading.

The journey had a triple purpose, really. It would bring her close to Seneca Falls, in time to accept an invitation from a sister temperance worker, Amelia Bloomer, and to hear two famous abolition speakers, Garrison and the Englishman, George Thompson. Mrs. Bloomer had even suggested the likelihood of encountering Elizabeth Cady Stanton in Seneca Falls, the sponsor of the franchise for women.

The meeting with Mrs. Stanton was too brief for Susan to discuss the pros and cons of female suffrage, but she had time to take in the bizarre, richly fashioned Bloomer costume, worn with considerable dash, and the dynamic personality of its wearer. Beside young Mrs. Stanton she felt suddenly drab and colorless. When Elizabeth Cady Stanton entered a room or walked onto a platform, Susan was to experience, over and over, that sensation of being snuffed out. It was quickly effaced now by the other woman's charm, lively humor and the warmth of her welcome.

A few weeks later Susan was back again in Seneca Falls, at Elizabeth's invitation, to meet Horace Greeley of the New York *Tribune* and Lucy Stone. The purpose of getting together was to discuss the possibility of a People's College which would admit women on an equal footing with men. The idea died later from lack of support, but the meeting gave Susan her chance to question both women at length on the movement in which they were pioneering.

The two fascinated her by their contrast. Their faith in the rightness of their cause, based on backgrounds and experience so different from each other and from her own, helped to remove a number of her doubts.

Although Susan attended every woman's rights convention she could after that, she went back to her chosen temperance work. But overbearing conceit of the Brothers of Temperance toward women workers soon proved too much for her, so she organized a Woman's Temperance Society which was to have no affiliation with the men's organization. Elizabeth Cady Stanton gave it her moral backing and became its nominal head.

It had, in consequence, a brief and stormy history. Elizabeth's leadership was always more bold than discreet. Advocating divorce, even for the valid reason of freeing women from confirmed drunkards, was too new and shocking an idea for Victorian standards. It caused so much argument within the society itself that Susan and Elizabeth finally resigned. Minus the only elements which had given it vitality, the group soon disintegrated, and women did not organize for temperance again until twenty years later, under the title **Woman's Christian Temperance Union.**

EIGHT

Having been an underpaid teacher herself, Susan tried next to better the lot of her sisters in the profession. But women were allowed no more voice in teachers' conventions than at temperance meetings, even though they greatly outnumbered the men.

At a convention in Rochester where, as usual, a small masculine minority had held undisputed possession of the floor from the start, Susan made up her mind to speak to the question then under debate: "Why is the profession of teacher less respected than that of lawyer, doctor or minister?"

After hours of discussion, in which of course only the men took part, Susan suddenly rose.

"Mr. President," she said.

At the unexpected sound of a woman's voice, an instant hush settled on the hall. Everyone turned in his seat to stare. With withering politeness the chairman wished to know what the lady would have? "I wish to speak to the question," replied Susan stoutly though her knees shook.

Instead of giving her the floor, the chairman turned the decision over to the convention, whereupon a babble of disagreement arose. Susan stood through the uproar until her right of free speech was finally conceded.

"It seems to me," she remarked quietly then, "that you fail to comprehend the cause of the disrespect you complain of. So long as society says woman has not brains enough to be a doctor, lawyer or minister, but has plenty to be a teacher, every man of you who condescends to teach tacitly admits before all Israel and the sun that he has no more brains than a woman."

In the moment of stunned surprise which followed, everyone had time to digest this acid truth. The meeting soon adjourned. The hardest lesson Susan had to learn at such times was that most women were content with society's verdict. They threw hostile looks at her now as they filed out of the hall, while her "disgraceful scene" was deplored with much tongue-clucking. However, Susan's stand was not wasted on the few who came up to grasp her hand, who admitted, "You have taught us a lesson." They remained staunch supporters of the reforms she continued to push for equal treatment of women teachers, until signal changes were made.

Multiplying experiences such as these convinced Susan that no actual betterment for women would be achieved until they were educated to use the vote in their own behalf. Although her interest in temperance, abolition and the field of education did not abate, she was ready at last to give herself heart and soul to winning the ballot.

One step toward this goal was to change the laws in New York State, which denied mothers control over their children and forced employers to hand a woman's wages over to her husband. Appeals to the State legislature became Elizabeth

SUSAN B. ANTHONY

Cady Stanton's special work, but these had to be backed up
by petitions signed by thousands of women, a staggering assignment which Susan undertook singlehanded.

In five short months she canvassed fifty-four counties in
New York, distributing tracts, speaking wherever she could
and gathering signatures for the petitions. It was winter, and
Susan traveled in jerky, sooty, one-track trains whose cars
were heated by potbellied stoves, or in open sleighs.

Once she caught a severe chill in her back. Unable to move,
she had herself carried to her sleigh and drove seventeen miles
to the next assignment, doubled up with pain. Iron resolve
pulled her through that meeting, but in the evening she decided to try an old country remedy guaranteed to kill or
cure. Buckets of ice water were poured over her back, after
which she was smothered in hot blankets. The next morning
she was alive—and well!

A rich Quaker courted Susan persistently on one stretch
of this particularly arduous campaign. His handsome sleigh,
equipped with footwarmers and fur robes, waited for her outside the halls where she spoke. He begged to be allowed to
drive her to this town and that village; he made advance
arrangements for her meetings; he even persuaded her to be
his guest in the fine home in which he lived with his sister.
It was, Susan politely admitted, a pleasant relief from the
chilly squalor of country hotels and farm houses and the
ordeal of plodding knee-deep through snowdrifts. But when
she had covered the district she left him disconsolate among
his riches, still more devoted to her cause than she could be
to any man, still preferring a hard life and independence to
the cushioned existence he offered.

Susan had no funds for this self-appointed work, and it was now she drew on the few hundred dollars she had once loaned her father and which he had returned. She did not know what it was to hesitate because the outcome looked hopeless or because there was no money. When something needed to be done, conviction drove her forward. She started on a long campaign once with only fifty dollars in her purse—and that loaned by her friend Wendell Phillips. Because a woman speaker in those days was almost as startling a novelty as a steam locomotive, country people were willing to drive miles and to pay a small fee to hear her. As a rule, she came back with expenses paid and enough to reimburse the donors.

Spreading the gospel of woman's rights in this manner was slow and disheartening work, but Susan like Lucy Stone, her fellow pioneer in Massachusetts, had the needed faith and the seed she planted did not die.

Trudging from house to house with an ever-shabbier suitcase loaded with the tracts she and Elizabeth composed between campaigns, Susan wore out her shoes and her bonnets and shawls, no longer either beribboned or gay. The women whose doorbells she rang had never heard of a petition, much less signed anything more important than a letter. But they knew this much—that her talk would make their husbands furious and arouse the minister's ire and the neighbors' ridicule. Often they slammed the door in her face.

But there were homes where she was invited in, where some woman's courage was revived before she left, where she made one more greatly needed convert, secured one more signature.

NINE

Susan was thirty-five now. One of the few favorable newspaper accounts of her at this time, written by the editor of a country paper, assured Victorian readers of her eminent respectability. "Miss Anthony put her decorous shawl on one chair, and a very exemplary bonnet on another, sat a moment, smoothed her hair discreetly, and then walked deliberately to the table and addressed the audience."

The delicate subject of Susan's spinsterhood it handled with tact: "She appears to be somewhere about the confines of the fourth luster in age." She had "pleasing rather than pretty features," an "expressive countenance," "rich brown hair effectively arranged," and was neither tall, short, plump nor thin. According to the editor she was "in brief, one of those *juste milieu* persons, the perfection of common sense physically exhibited."

The press was always stilted but rarely so chivalrous. The Utica *Evening Telegram*, besides dubbing her a "shrewish maiden," added this spiteful comment: "Personally repulsive, she seems to be laboring under feelings of strong hatred towards male men, the effect we presume of jealousy and neglect." Now that the research of psychoanalysts has invented as much and presumed a great deal more about Susan and her sister pioneers, it can even be said that she got off easily in her day.

As a matter of fact, few spinsters of Susan's day enjoyed her free association and frank exchange with the opposite sex. Her fellow crusaders and her opponents were the ablest men of her generation. Emerson, Theodore Parker, Thomas Wentworth Higginson, Garrison, Wendell Phillips, Horace Greeley, William Henry Channing were only a few of the illustrious brotherhood and the equally illustrious opposition.

Some of them were not above throwing her spinsterhood in her face. When she and Elizabeth Cady Stanton startled society with their now-famous demand for more liberal divorce laws, the Reverend A. H. Mayo, an abolitionist and up to then a believer in woman's rights, turned on Susan with the crushing reminder:

"You are not married. You have no business to be discussing marriage."

"Well, Mr. Mayo," Susan's eyebrows lifted in mild amusement, "you are not a slave. Suppose you quit lecturing on slavery."

Susan, it must be confessed, had moments of desperation when she feared marriage might undo the Cause. One after another, Antoinette Brown and Lucy Stone were caught up in what she ruefully described as "the mighty matrimonial maelstrom." Elizabeth Cady Stanton, with her steadily growing family, was frequently forced to curtail her efforts for woman's rights. It often seemed to Susan that she held the fort alone, especially when a convention date arrived and her chief drawing cards, the prominent crusaders on whose eloquence she had always been able to count, began to default for family reasons. A baby was on the way, or a wife had to accompany her husband on a trip, or the canning season was on.

During this period, Susan, who always spoke reluctantly and had never been able to memorize any speech, was often forced to pinch-hit. The necessity developed an apt and forceful speaker though it never ceased to be "martyrdom"; and worry for the movement haunted her. Where was the old fervor that had once launched the Cause? A great principle was at stake and while its fate hung in the balance women were allowing themselves to get enmeshed again in the familiar domestic pattern.

From time immemorial men had renounced home life and family joys for public service; women could not hope to escape the same obligation. Sole arbiter of her own life, Susan gave herself to the Cause with the devotion of a zealot, and was both shocked and disappointed when Antoinette and Lucy gave in to masculine persuasion.

To Elizabeth she poured out all her impatience without fear of being misunderstood. The Stanton house at Seneca Falls had become a second home to Susan; the Stanton children adopted nephews and nieces whom she scolded and loved, washed and fed, while their mother snatched a few quiet hours in which to think through her next attack on the New York legislature.

Without "Aunt Susan" to take over household responsibilities when an emergency arose in the defense of woman's rights, most of Elizabeth's epoch-making addresses would have remained unwritten, and without Elizabeth's unfailing encouragement and resourceful wit when it was Susan who needed support, women might have waited a century longer for their freedoms.

In the house in Seneca Falls a friendship was being cemented that was rare among women at that time. None of the ordinary and usually very personal feminine reasons for friendship fitted their case. It was founded on a political principle and a shared passion for freedom. Amenities flew up the chimney in their heated and endless debates over woman's destiny by Elizabeth's fireside, after the Stanton children were in bed. The partnership was to weather their own strong wills, their completely opposite temperaments, and the inevitable envy of smaller people.

As time went on, both the press and the public were better able to estimate their stature and importance in history. Susan's executive gifts and tireless campaigning earned her the title "Napoleon" of the movement. Elizabeth was its acknowledged mouthpiece.

TEN

By this time mounting tension over the slavery issue had pulled Susan into the abolition ranks. She was too able an organizer to escape the notice of the Garrison Anti-Slavery Society, and they wrote her a flattering letter to that effect. Susan agreed to manage a number of speaking tours for them during the three years preceding the Civil War.

She had always felt that sooner or later she would be drawn into the abolition fight; ever since those Sunday night suppers at home when Frederick Douglass, Garrison and Wendell Phillips had turned a young schoolmarm into an agitator.

Only recently her younger brother Merritt, who had settled in Kansas, had joined the conflict there between free-soilers and proslavery Missourians. Merritt had sheltered John Brown under his own roof and fought by his side during the famous raid at Osawatomie. The call to action for Susan was inescapable.

Southern threats to secede from the Union had by this time greatly intensified feeling in the North. Shepherding her band of antislavery speakers through the New York towns in which she had a short while ago campaigned for woman's rights, Susan faced mob violence. Most of her meetings were broken up by gangs. In Syracuse her effigy and those of other speakers were dragged through the streets and burned in the square. The only police protection she received on the entire tour was given her by the courageous Albany Mayor who sat on the platform with a drawn revolver.

But abolitionists could not harness a woman to a single cause, as they had already found to their chagrin. Lucy Stone had struck blows for woman's rights during her antislavery talks, and Lucretia Mott had fought for the dignity of woman at the World Anti-Slavery Convention in London.

Susan had already become acquainted with the famous Mott family. During a Woman's Rights Convention in Philadelphia, she had been one of twenty-four delegates invited by Lucretia and James to stay in their home. On this occasion Susan had been an honored guest, sitting on Lucretia's left opposite Garrison. She had dried the silver and choice pieces of china and glass which her hostess always washed in a small cedar tub of hot water, brought to the table while the good talk went on.

Now, five years later, while in the midst of antislavery work, Susan visited Lydia Mott, sister of James, in Albany. On an errand one day, the two were accosted by a strange woman, her face hidden behind thick veils. In Lydia's home she told a story which inspired Susan to one of those intrepid and chivalrous acts in defense of women which her fellow abolitionists so deplored.

The veiled woman proved to be Mrs. Charles Abner Phelps, wife of a prominent Massachusetts legislator. She had one day faced her husband with proof of his infidelities, and he, in a dangerous fit of rage, had thrown her down a flight of stairs. When violence neither killed her nor silenced her threats of exposure, he had her committed to an insane asylum, an easy way to be rid of troublesome relatives at that period.

She remained there for eighteen months, until her brother, a United States Senator, bestirred himself sufficiently to obtain his sister's release by habeas corpus writ and took her to his home. But Mrs. Phelps had three children still under her husband's roof. After much pleading and as a great concession they were allowed to visit their mother for a few weeks. When the father demanded their return she begged to be allowed to keep her little girl.

This request was considered quite unreasonable, even by her family. Did she not realize that children, under Massachusetts law, were the property of the father? She could either submit, or, her brother suggested, be returned to the asylum.

Meanwhile, rumors of a Miss Anthony who was waging a stubborn fight for woman's rights had reached the ears of the desperate mother. She fled her brother's house, taking her daughter with her, and set out to find Susan. Hiding wherever people were willing to give her and the child shelter, she at last located her in Albany.

Her tale was so lurid that Susan must have listened with just a shade of doubt.

"Here are the names of friends who will vouch for me," the woman pleaded urgently. "They can tell you that before my marriage I was principal of a school, and I have written a number of books."

Perhaps it was at Lydia Mott's sensible advice that Susan

did investigate. The friends of Mrs. Phelps confirmed her story but would not help. The family was too prominent. No one wished to interfere. Susan grew more and more indignant, and meantime both the brother and husband were conducting a search for the child who had disappeared with her mother.

On the afternoon of December 25, Susan boarded a train, southbound to New York from Albany. She placed herself near a poor working woman who wore dark spectacles. Beside her sat a shabbily dressed little girl. Arriving in the city the three made their way to a hotel.

The clerk eyed the queer-looking trio suspiciously. "We don't take ladies unaccompanied by gentlemen," he stated firmly.

The next hotel made the same excuse.

Remembering an acquaintance who kept a boarding house, Susan went there, but the woman became frightened.

"If it should leak out that I have harbored a runaway wife my business will be ruined," she pleaded.

There was nothing for it but go out again into the storm. They had not enough money for cabs now. The driving snow and the drifts through which they stumbled soaked their clothes and chilled them.

"Sorry, we are filled up," was the answer at the next hotel, but it had too familiar a sound.

"I know," replied Susan, "that that isn't so. Either give us a place to sleep or we shall sit in the lobby."

"Madam, I should regret having to call the police."

"Do so," retorted Susan. "We shall at least be dry here until they come."

"Capable of making a scene," was the manager's mental note. He preferred giving them a room, but it was fireless and they were unable to dry their clothing.

Susan spent the whole of the next day tramping the streets with her charges to find them temporary shelter. No one was eager for the certain notoriety when Mrs. Phelps's identity should be discovered. Finally a friend more courageous than the rest took them in, and Susan went back to Albany to her antislavery work—in itself a risky occupation—and to the threatening letters which shortly arrived from Mr. Phelps, demanding to know the whereabouts of his child and wife.

He had got wind of the fact that Susan was responsible for their disappearance. She would pay dearly for her lawbreaking, he assured her. He would sue.

"I propose to defy the law and you also," was Susan's answer. "There is no reason or justice in woman's submitting to such outrages."

In hiding, under an assumed name, and under the protection of a charity organization, Mrs. Phelps eked out a bare existence as a seamstress. Her income from her books was quickly confiscated by her husband, who notified publishers to send all further payments to him. Massachusetts law not only made this theft legal, but when a year later the child was snatched off the city streets by agents of the father, the mother never recovered her.

Meanwhile Susan's name was linked to the whole publicized affair. And her name was widely known by now, as well as her affiliation with the abolition society. Garrison and Phillips thought her act ill-advised and legally untenable. It would strengthen the claim that abolitionists were a lawless band. Their letters urging her to retract her position had the force and weight of men who never retracted themselves or minced words.

Their stern disapproval nearly broke Susan. They were the finest men she knew. But she stuck to her guns.

"United States law gives the slaveholder ownership of the slave and you break that law every time you help a slave into Canada, don't you?" she defied Garrison.

"Yes, I do."

"Well, the law which gives the father sole ownership of children is just as wicked and I'll break it just as quickly. You would die before you would deliver a slave to its master, and I will die before I give up that child to its father."

Daniel Anthony, who had endangered a livelihood more than once for his sense of right, now risked the estrangement of old friends. "My child, don't put a word on paper or make a statement that you are not prepared to make in court," he wrote her from Rochester. "Legally you are wrong, but morally you are right. I will stand by you." The entire world might rock on its foundations, but not Daniel and his principles, thought Susan, pride in him suddenly blurring the words she read.

As it turned out, the men of the Phelps family were too much in public life to wish to sue. It suited them better to have agents quietly kidnap the child.

ELEVEN

The Civil War broke soon after this incident and while women's attention was diverted to war work, New York legislators repealed the recent law which had given mothers of the Empire State equal guardianship of their children. Had such a law existed in Massachusetts the Phelps drama could never have been enacted.

This Equal Guardianship Bill was one of the measures for which Susan had been gathering petitions up and down the whole length and breadth of the state and for which Elizabeth Cady Stanton had made her famous plea before the State Judiciary Committee. The crowning achievement of several years' work was thus wiped out in one unguarded moment. It was a stunning blow, but Susan rallied with her usual spirit. "We deserve to suffer for our confidence in man's sense of justice," she concluded.

In the midst of Civil War tensions Susan received the shocking news of Daniel's sudden death. The father whose unflinching ideals had shaped her own had been her closest friend. She labored on in the reforms he too had supported, but with an aching sense of loss. During this period she and

Elizabeth Cady Stanton, working together as they so often did, became leaders of the Woman's National Loyal League, formed to rally the opinion of women behind postwar reforms.

At the end of the Civil War came that letter from Lucy Stone and her husband Henry Blackwell, begging Elizabeth and Susan to follow up the gains she and Henry had made for woman suffrage in Kansas.

Elated at the prospect of working so fertile an area, the two women set forth. The trip was to prove a grilling test of friendship.

Susan was already inured to poor food, bad air, the grime and soot of primitive rail travel, the fatigue of horse-drawn journeys, vile cooking and bedbugs. Considering Elizabeth had never been hardened to real discomforts, she stood it amazingly.

Susan was Spartan in her habits and a hardheaded realist; Elizabeth was luxury-loving and temperamental. Susan's few belongings never got mislaid; Elizabeth strewed their journey with forgotten handkerchiefs, gloves and toilet articles.

Susan went into action as soon as they reached a town. She engaged the halls, swept them when she had to, saw to the lighting and chairs, posted announcements, sold tickets at the door, started the meetings, introduced the speakers—all with scarcely a pause to wash off the dust of her journey.

Elizabeth appeared after the arrangements were made, refreshed and well-groomed. Her hair was in perfect curl. She had been given time to bathe, nap and change her clothes. Ready to do battle, her shrewd little eyes twinkled with the humor and zest her audiences loved.

Susan accepted her thankless job without a murmur. Elizabeth was the luminary in the sky of Woman's Rights. Her function was to shine, as Susan's was to drudge. Together they made an unbeatable pair, but the same uncalculating devotion to the Cause could lead Susan into some curious errors of judgment, one of the most startling being her association with George Francis Train.

In the coming elections, Republicans were openly opposing the amendment for woman suffrage. The only hope lay in winning over the Democratic party, and this Train proposed to do by joining their campaign, he told Susan.

If it was true that Train was seeking new ways to exploit himself, he was also known to be a brilliant speaker. Susan accepted him with hardly a qualm.

When all the other men were deserting woman for what they called the Negro's prior claim, was this the time to spurn a knight-errant with money to burn?

Train's oddities grew more astonishing with acquaintance, but so did his virtues. He took his audiences by storm, he had impeccable manners and a chivalrous vein. To Susan, moreover, he was that rarest of all species—"a total abstinence man."

At the start, she was afraid he might default like other ordinary males. A volunteer speaker, Mr. Reynolds, had soon found Elizabeth and Susan's pace too strenuous. Train himself, on examining the route one day, refused with a shudder to go a step farther. The trip they suggested to him was "too rough for any man," he asserted.

Susan looked him over coldly. "The halls have been engaged, Mr. Train, and the handbills sent to every post office within fifty miles of where we shall speak. I am taking Mr.

Reynolds' place. At one o'clock I shall send the carriage to your hotel. You can do as you please about going. If you decline I shall conduct the meetings alone."

Mr. Train bowed with his inimitable flourish. "You make a man feel ashamed, Miss Anthony."

Thereafter, he followed wherever the undaunted Miss Anthony led. His last act disarmed Susan completely, fulfilling as it did her long-cherished dream of a weekly for the suffrage movement.

She accepted in good faith Train's advance of three thousand dollars, and his promise of a hundred thousand more. She also innocently agreed to let him advertise some very questionable financial schemes in *The Revolution.* In New York, and especially in Wall Street circles, the news spread that Train was a charlatan. He soon vanished abroad on new visionary adventure and his support of the paper likewise vanished.

When *The Revolution* finally collapsed after Susan's heroic struggle to keep it going, she sold it for a dollar and found herself owing ten thousand dollars. This staggering debt she paid off in six years by constant lecturing, a feat which astounded men she knew, who would themselves have chosen bankruptcy and left their creditors to do the worrying.

A twelve-months' speaking tour that wound up in California became part of Susan's debt-lifting program. It was also her first campaign for woman's rights in the far West. During this year Susan delivered 171 lectures, besides hundreds of impromptu talks. She traveled ceaselessly.

The journey home through the Rockies in January became rugged when her train ran into mountainous drifts. Tracks

had been recently laid, breakdowns were frequent and waits
interminable. Passengers had nothing to eat but the cold food
they had had the foresight to bring. Many nights were spent
sitting bolt upright.

Susan did get back finally, in time for the annual convention
of her National Woman Suffrage Association in the capital.

"You must be tired," they greeted her in Washington.

"Why, what should make me tired?" asked Susan. "I
haven't been doing anything for two weeks."

The restfulness of transcontinental rail trips in the 1870's
was not apparent to others and was soon forgotten by Susan
in the stress of the next few weeks. Shortly afterwards, she
became the defendant in a bitterly fought dispute with the
government of the United States.

TWELVE

A St. Louis lawyer by the name of Francis Minor had suddenly raised a question about the Constitution which seemed very important to women. The first clause of the Fourteenth Amendment, Minor claimed, automatically enfranchised them. In it, citizens were defined as "all persons born or naturalized in the United States" and subject to its laws. No sex qualification was added until the second clause.

It followed logically that the newly passed Fifteenth Amendment, granting voting rights to citizens which must not be "denied or abridged on account of race, color or previous condition of servitude," referred to the rights of women as well as men. A number of lawyers agreed that the law might be so construed. The next step was to bring it to the attention of Congress.

Accordingly, Susan, Elizabeth Cady Stanton and Isabella Beecher Hooker went before the Senate Judiciary Committee and presented the following resolution:

"As the Fourteenth and Fifteenth Amendments to the Constitution have established the right of women to the elective franchise, we demand of the present Congress a declaratory act which shall secure us at once in the exercise of this right."

But the Senate Judiciary Committee refused to admit such an interpretation or to present the demand to Congress. Clearly, unless a legal decision was compelled, the matter would never be settled.

Elections were approaching and Susan decided there was no better time for a showdown. She went home to Rochester and, accompanied by two of her sisters, presented herself at the polling center to register. Rochester inspectors were dumfounded and uncertain whether to accept the names of the three women, but Susan had come armed with a copy of the Constitution. The amendments in question read so convincingly to the men that they allowed twelve other women (whom Susan had rounded up) to register.

Next morning Rochester papers carried the news and some demanded the arrest of the inspectors of election. Susan was too used to the ranting of the press to be concerned. She had consulted Judge Henry R. Selden, an eminent lawyer in Rochester, who agreed that the legal odds were greatly in her favor and that a test case was the only way to prove it. Next day Susan, and the other women who had registered in the same precinct with her, voted without hindrance.

Two weeks went by. On Thanksgiving day the Anthony doorbell rang and Susan was told a gentleman waited in the parlor to see her. Her visitor was imposingly tall and formally attired, but he twirled his high beaver hat uneasily.

"Miss Anthony—" he began, and then became speechless.

"Won't you sit down?" Susan offered him a chair politely.

"No, thank you. You see," he stammered, "I am here, Miss

Anthony, on a most uncomfortable errand. The fact is"—the gentleman's discomfort was now acute—"I have come to arrest you."

"Arrest me?" said Susan. The possibility had not occurred to her.

"If you will oblige me by coming as soon as possible to the District Attorney's office, no escort will be necessary," and the Deputy Marshal of Rochester tried to edge himself gracefully out of the parlor.

But Susan got to the door first. "Is this the usual manner of serving a warrant?" she asked quietly.

Blushing absurdly, the Marshal drew the document from his pocket and waited while Susan read the charge against her. She had voted without having a lawful right to vote and in violation of Section 19 of an Act of Congress, entitled: "An act to enforce the right of citizens of the United States to vote in the several states of this Union and for other purposes."

Susan turned to her visitor again. "I prefer to be arrested like everybody else. You may handcuff me as soon as I get my coat and hat." She was gone before he could answer.

The Deputy Marshal had imagined every embarrassment but this. He insisted that he had left these implements of his office behind, and so, escorted but not handcuffed by her reluctant captor, Susan at last stood before the District Attorney.

With immense gravity he proceeded with his examination. "Previous to voting at the First District poll in the Eighth Ward, did you take the advice of counsel upon your voting?"

"Yes, sir."

"Who was it you talked with?"

"Judge Henry Selden."

"What did he advise you in reference to your legal right to vote?"

"He said it was the only way to find out what the law was upon the subject, to bring it to a test case."

"Did he advise you to offer your vote?"

"Yes, sir."

"State whether or not prior to such advice, you had retained Mr. Selden."

"No, sir."

"Have you anything further to say upon Judge Selden's advice?"

"I think it was sound."

"Did he give you an opinion on the subject?"

"He was like the rest of you lawyers, he had not studied the question."

"What did he advise you?"

"He left me with this opinion: that he was a conscientious man; that he would thoroughly study the subject of woman's right to vote and decide according to law."

"Did you have any doubt yourself of your right to vote?"

"Not a particle."

At the second hearing, soon after this, Susan, the other women who had voted with her, and the three inspectors who permitted the crime, were declared guilty of violating the Constitution. The case of the United States vs. Susan B. Anthony was on.

All involved gave bail and were released, pending their trial, but Susan applied for a writ of habeas corpus. This was denied her by the District Judge who promptly doubled her bail. Thoroughly angry by now, Susan refused to pay, but her attorney, Judge Selden, shocked by the alternative of jail for a gentlewoman, advanced the necessary sum.

It was a gallant but unfortunate gesture. By not going to jail, Susan forfeited her right to carry her case to the Supreme Court as she was intending to do. The technicality was not brought to her attention until it was too late to cancel her bail.

At liberty now until the date of her trial, Susan took her case to the people of New York by lecturing up and down the state on "Is It a Crime for a United States Citizen to Vote?" She rallied enough favorable opinion to worry the District Attorney. By the time the date of her trial occurred, the case was being widely discussed. Government prosecutors chose to hold court in the remote village of Canandaigua.

Justice Ward Hunt, on the bench, after listening to the arguments of Susan's lawyer, Judge Selden, and of the opposing District Attorney, immediately submitted a written opinion that the Fourteenth and Fifteenth Amendments could not be construed as giving women the right to vote. This was his first legal impropriety.

He had obviously formed his opinion before hearing the arguments.

His next was to instruct the jury to render a verdict of guilty. When Judge Selden objected and demanded that the jury be polled, he dismissed the jury.

"Has the prisoner anything to say why sentence should not be pronounced?" inquired Justice Hunt then.

"Your Honor, I have many things to say," replied Susan. "In your ordered verdict of guilty you have trampled on my natural rights, my civil rights, my political rights, my judicial rights and have degraded me from the status of a citizen to that of a subject—"

"The Court cannot listen to a rehearsal of argument which the prisoner's counsel has already consumed three hours in presenting."

"May it please your Honor, I am not arguing the question but stating the reasons why sentence cannot in justice be pronounced—"

"The Court cannot allow the prisoner to go on."

"Your Honor's denial of my citizen's right to vote is the denial of my right of consent as one of the governed, the denial of my right of representation as one of the taxed, the denial of my right to trial by a jury of my peers; therefore the denial of my sacred right to life, liberty, property and—"

"The prisoner must sit down—the Court cannot allow it."

But the prisoner went on, even though she was interrupted three more times, ordered to sit down, and told the Court would "not allow another word."

Only after she had said all that was on her mind did Justice Hunt really get the floor.

"The prisoner will stand up. The sentence of the Court is that you pay a fine of a hundred dollars, and the costs of the prosecution."

"May it please your Honor," said Susan, "I will never pay a dollar of your unjust penalty."

She kept her word. Knowing very well that if he held her until she did pay, Susan would instantly appeal to a higher court, the judge let her go. The other women involved were never brought to trial and the three inspectors of election, defended by John Van Voorhis, were sentenced and fined in the same court as Susan and in the same highhanded manner. Some of the jury were heard to say later that they would have rendered a verdict of "not guilty."

Friends, and even strangers, indignant over the mistrial, dug into their pockets to defray the court costs of the inspectors. The two lawyers, Selden and Van Voorhis, gave their services and the fines of the inspectors were finally cancelled by President Grant.

A legal decision had now been rendered and precedent established that it was illegal for women to vote.

"There never was a trial in the country of one half the importance of this of Miss Anthony's," said John Van Voorhis twenty years later. "That of Andrew Jackson had no issue which could compare in value with the one here at stake. If Miss Anthony had won her case on the merits, it would have revolutionized the suffrage of the country and enfranchised every woman in the United States. There was a prearranged determination to convict her. A jury trial was dangerous, and so the Constitution was openly and deliberately violated."

Three years later, Mrs. Minor, wife of the lawyer who had first brought up the question, voted, and succeeded in carrying her case to the Supreme Court. There, too, the officiating Judge rendered an adverse decision. The hope that female suffrage might be conceded on existing law vanished.

THIRTEEN

Prospects for winning the franchise might have seemed more hopeless than ever now but for one ray of light in the gloom. The Territory of Wyoming had recently adopted woman suffrage!

Soon after her trial, Susan set out alone to stump the Territory of Colorado. Obviously, it was in pioneer soil among settlers that revolutionary ideas flourished best. There were few traditions to combat in Colorado, and, as she soon learned, no conventions worth mentioning.

Squatters, derelicts, miners and gold prospectors were her traveling companions and made up most of her audiences. Hotels were little more than shacks; beds a few planks covered with straw ticking. One memorable night, Susan found six carousing gold diggers in the hotel room next to hers. The only wall between was a thin wooden partition reaching halfway to the ceiling. Locks on doors were unheard of.

She held meetings in railroad stations, saloons or any other shelter that was offered her. The men had their own ideas of what was due a lady speaker. When Susan coughed in the smoke-laden air, they obligingly knocked out their pipes and drowned their craving for tobacco in more whiskey.

Other speakers were to follow Susan into Colorado, but she broke ground in the toughest district and when the state became the second to enfranchise women, she felt repaid for the hardest of all her campaigns.

FOURTEEN

"I shall never again beg my rights, but will come to Congress each year and demand recognition of them," Susan had declared after her trial.

It was an appointment she never missed. Susan's persistence was as patient and stubborn as water that wears away stone. It was essentially a feminine weapon. Persistence became the irresistible power behind the suffrage forces, and these were growing, in spite of scathing ridicule, into a body important enough to be dubbed "the shrieking sisterhood."

All the movement's leaders, people firmly believed, were clownish spinsters or childless wives. Susan knew herself to be the most frequently cited example. The following anonymous telegram, circulated around the country, was typical. It described her arrival at a convention.

"Miss Anthony stalked down the aisle with faded alpaca dress to the top of her boots, blue cotton umbrella and white cotton gloves, perched herself on the platform, crossed her legs, pulled out her snuffbox and passed it around. On the platform were

Mrs. Stanton, Mrs. Wright, Mrs. Gage, Mrs. Rose
and other noted women, all dressed in unmention-
ables cut bias, and smoking penny-drab cigars.
Susan was quite drunk."

As a matter of fact, sixteen of the most prominent suffragists at this time were exemplary wives and devoted mothers,
with a total among them of sixty-six children.

Actually, there were enough able women in the movement
now to allow Susan and Elizabeth to begin their long-planned
project—*The History of Woman Suffrage.*

Susan arrived at the Stanton home for a prolonged stay and
to labor daily with Elizabeth in her library. The litter the
two confronted from twenty years of accumulated files would
have frightened weaker souls. However, no one else could
help, because no one alive now remembered so well the birth
throes of the movement. The discord of their united effort
surprised no one in the household, used for years to the arguments of "Mother and Aunt Susan."

After the first two volumes were ready for the press, Mrs.
Stanton was ready for a rest. So was Susan, only it was Elizabeth, as usual, who took it. She stayed in Europe for a good
deal more than the few months she had promised, urging
Susan meanwhile to join her in England for a well-earned
vacation.

It was just like Elizabeth to think the Cause could drift on
without direction and that she, Susan, could suddenly drop
the reins in someone else's lap, Susan grumbled to herself.
Elizabeth had always gone her free untrammeled way, crusading for various side issues that caught her enthusiasm, punc-

turing smug virtue wherever she found it and with special glee taking pot shots at the bigotry of the clergy.

Not that Susan didn't stoutly support all these independent forays, especially when Elizabeth was criticized; only her inseparable ally sometimes tried her patience to the breaking point. For thirty years Susan had spent hardly a cent on herself; the habit of putting the Cause first had become ingrained. She brushed aside the thought of a trip to Europe as impossible.

But the justice of a respite for the woman, who at sixty-three was still giving herself unsparingly to an ideal, began to circulate among fellow workers and friends. It gathered momentum. Soon because no one else thought it incredible, Susan herself had to admit that the way was opening.

A young, and devoted follower declared she was going abroad for study; if Miss Anthony would come along, she would manage the whole journey. Susan would be waited on for a change—no arrangements to make, no tickets to buy, no rooms to engage! The temptation was irresistible.

As soon as it was known that Susan B. Anthony was leaving the country, affectionate tributes from all over the nation poured in. Especially warming were telegrams from old friends like Wendell Phillips and Frederick Douglass from whom she had been estranged. Gifts and remembrances arrived. A diaphanous fichu of real lace from the people of Rochester, a steamer rug, a traveling bag, a gold-handled umbrella, a silver traveling cup, rich satin material for a dress, and from one of those masculine admirers who were so much in the background of Susan's life, a hundred-dollar check with the note:

"I don't believe in woman suffrage, but I do believe in Susan B. Anthony."

The money, the donor stated, was to be spent on an India shawl, the best to be had. Susan's unflagging labors had left their mark. Her hair was gray, her face worn, but she still loved finery. She obeyed him to the letter.

In the course of time she was presented with many shawls, but the famous one, which lies now in the Smithsonian Institution, in the capital, was a warm blood-red, the color of valor. She carried it so invariably that the public soon identified her by it. It grew in time to be a symbol, the battle flag, around which the Movement rallied.

Once at a huge convention she appeared without it. Newspapermen were the first to notice and protest. "No shawl— no report," they sent their ultimatum in a note to the platform where she sat. They had the satisfaction of provoking her rare laugh. "Am sending for it," she scribbled back, "immediately!"

On arriving in England, she discovered to her amazement that the name of Susan B. Anthony was well known. Elizabeth welcomed her with all the old warmth and the deviltry Susan loved. In London, she fell under the spell of Irving and Ellen Terry and Sarah Bernhardt. The Puritan in Susan had long since died. But for all she reveled in the Old World culture and art she was tasting for the first time, Susan the crusader fought undemocratic ways wherever she found them.

The feudalism which still flourished on the continent shocked her. In Germany, military swagger and masculine authority seemed particularly inflated, and women the special slaves of their husbands, their sons and their brothers.

In Germany, therefore, Susan was enormously pleased that she had brought along a plentiful supply of envelopes belonging to her National Woman Suffrage Association. They bore on their flaps, two good old American slogans: "No just government can be formed without the consent of the governed," and "Taxation without representation is tyranny."

Her letters were now speeded home in these envelopes and as speedily returned to the American Embassy in Berlin! "Such sentiments cannot pass through the post office in Germany," was the Bismarckian edict.

Returning to England again on her way home, she met all the important suffragists in London, spoke to an audience of two thousand, and, with Elizabeth Cady Stanton, was an honored guest at countless functions. A side trip into Scotland and Ireland followed, but in Ireland the wretched hovels in which the peasants lived spoiled most of her pleasure in the beauty of the country.

FIFTEEN

It was, on the whole, a more-than-willing Susan who returned to America on the same boat with Elizabeth Cady Stanton, after an absence of nine months. She came home refreshed, her mind and spirit enriched, indelible glories stamped on her memory; the Alps, the treasures of Florence and Rome, Grand Opera in Paris, the Louvre, and a few never-to-be-forgotten moments alone, at the tomb of Napoleon. She had also seen that women in Europe were more enslaved than in her own land. The dream of a great international awakening began to take shape in her mind.

On the long ocean voyage, Susan could not help reflecting that she had arrived in England none too soon to rescue Elizabeth from decay. Mrs. Stanton's life there had been gracious, leisurely, urbane; too full of ease for any crusader's good, and, alas, very much to her taste.

Many-faceted and gifted, she had been welcomed among progressive English thinkers, but the suffrage movement, in a country of deeply rooted traditions and where a Queen had made a cult of domesticity, was a pallid counterpart of that in America. Militancy was to come later, after Victoria's reign. Elizabeth had lost none of her revolutionary convictions in England, but Susan missed in her the old lust for work and battle.

Capricious and willful though she was, her will was no match for Susan's. On the journey home, the two were engaged in one of those silent but stubborn tussles that ended usually in Elizabeth's defeat. The third volume of *The History of Woman Suffrage* was long overdue. They must start work on it as soon as they got home. Susan had been harping on this unwelcome theme ever since she had arrived in London.

Elizabeth's prompt retreat, after she landed, to her childhood home in Johnstown, New York, availed her nothing. The remote quiet there made it an ideal spot for work, Susan pointed out, and shortly the trunks full of documents that remained to be sifted and used were hauled out of storage where they had been buried for the past months, and installed in Johnstown. The two plunged into incessant clashes of wit and frenzy of labor.

They were never again to be so closely associated or to enjoy each other more keenly. As soon as the volume was finished Elizabeth went back to England for another prolonged stay.

In January of the year 1886, a bill to enfranchise women was presented to the Senate for the first time and suffered its first defeat. In the coming years this same measure would be submitted to Congress regularly, until the number of congressmen favoring woman suffrage grew to a majority. Senator Henry W. Blair was the first to introduce it.

Susan by this time was a familiar figure in the capital. Her relations with Blair and other congressmen friendly to the woman's cause had the give and take common among political colleagues. During the weeks while Blair was negotiating to get the bill before the Senate, Susan was a lobbyist of the most persistent kind.

"I thought just as likely as not you would come fussing round," he wrote her a bantering note now to assure her he was pushing the issue as hard as he could. "I wish you would go home. I don't see what you want to meddle for, anyway." And as a final impudence, "Go off and get married!"

The resolution declaring that the "rights of citizens of the United States to vote shall not be denied or abridged on account of sex," was voted down in the Senate, but Susan was not discouraged. The willingness of a few congressmen to support the bill was in itself a preliminary victory.

She had, besides, another iron on the fire which had been growing hotter ever since her return from Europe. Of all her successful feats of propaganda and organization, Susan's calling of a great international congress of women to the capital was probably her masterpiece. Its cost was a fraction of the amount spent by men on a similar conclave that same year.

Appeals and calls went out to every part of the world. The number of letters, circulars, folders, pamphlets and booklets advertising the campaign and its delegates, and advising those coming about various methods of travel, was a huge enterprise in itself.

But detailed and immense as the project was, Susan's only acute worry was her arrangement with Elizabeth Cady Stanton.

The Congress was scheduled to open on the fortieth anniversary of the birth of the woman movement at Seneca Falls. Because Elizabeth had instigated that first meeting and originated the historic demand for the franchise, she was to be the chief exhibit. She was still in England. But she had promised to come back to address the Congress—and then she suddenly reneged.

"I'm ablaze with anger and dare not write tonight," Susan's diary records her shock on getting the news.

The next day she added: "I wrote the most terrific letter to Mrs. Stanton; it will start every white hair on her head."

The culprit yielded with good grace. She arrived barely in time to prepare a speech, but she never delivered a better one nor wrote one with more dispatch.

Susan's International Congress of Women in the spring of 1888 was the first of its kind. It forced recognition that an immense awakening was taking place among women. It also speeded the union of the suffrage workers in America, who had been so long estranged.

Susan had welcomed the chance to invite Lucy Stone, Henry Blackwell, Antoinette Brown and all the survivors of the original army of crusaders. The ranks were being depleted. Garrison and Phillips were gone, Douglass was an ill man. Those who were able to come spoke movingly. The assemblage from foreign lands learned that the greater freedom of women in America had been won through fiery conflict. As the pioneers described their early struggles and told of their common persecutions, the glow of comradeship was rekindled.

Many years had passed since they had all stood together on a platform. The move, already started, to unite the two Woman Suffrage Associations was made easier by this first gesture of reconciliation. In the following year the union was accomplished.

Although it had been agreed, in order to avoid factional feeling, that none of the original leaders should head the newly merged organization, it was found impossible to rally the movement around lesser figures. While the three great pioneers lived, they would continue to capture the imagination of the public and hold the allegiances they had won.

Elizabeth Cady Stanton became President, Susan B. Anthony Vice-President-at-Large, and Lucy Stone Chairman of the Executive Committee of the National American Woman Suffrage Association.

Elizabeth's position was mainly honorary. From now on she concerned herself less and less with the movement. Her campaigning was a thing of the past.

Not so with Susan, who at seventy went blithely off on a campaign in South Dakota where Indian raids were still a recent memory. For exertion and hardship, this one equaled her most strenuous campaigns. In South Dakota, however, she had the able support of two young enthusiasts. One was Carrie Chapman Catt, the other, Anna Howard Shaw. Both succeeded her eventually in leadership of the Movement.

After so many years on the road, Susan longed for a home. At the same time, it was beginning to seem more and more possible, and even wise, to let the younger workers feel the full weight of their coming task.

Meanwhile, Susan's mother and all her sisters had died save Mary, the youngest. The two were deeply attached, so it was a happy decision for them both now to share a home together in Rochester.

Elizabeth Cady Stanton, who had given up her home and knew what it was to feel uprooted and adrift, highly approved the plan for Susan.

"I rejoice that you are going to housekeeping," she wrote, adding characteristically, "My advice to you, Susan, is to keep some spot you can call your own; where you can live and die in peace and be cremated in your own oven if you desire."

In the congenial atmosphere of home, and between campaigns and conventions that required her presence, Susan kept up her vast correspondence with suffrage workers all over the country. She was still the driving spirit behind the organization, and there were, besides, local causes that needed her courageous championing.

A State Industrial School in Rochester—a reformatory for young people—was a case in point. In arresting boys and girls for misconduct, the police always sent the boys home and held the girls. In court, the boys were made to come merely to testify against the girls, after which they were released without even a reprimand. The girls were sent to the reformatory.

The custom of condoning male immorality and punishing the female offender was older than any law. Susan and Elizabeth had fought it before with little success. Susan's protest now made no impression on the police in Rochester. At the reformatory itself there were minor injustices that no one but Susan sought to abolish. The boys were given the use of the steam laundry, while the girls had to break their backs over old-fashioned tubs. Efforts were made to re-educate the boys but the girls were ignored.

Another fight, launched by Susan after making her home in Rochester, was for coeducation at the University of Rochester. The raising of sufficient funds for a girls' department was one of the last campaigns she initiated.

Now that she could spare some time from the suffrage movement, Susan's affection and concern for young people found wider expression. She had always won them easily with her fairness and honesty. Her comradeship with one young niece and namesake, "Susan B.," had been a specially treasured tie. But Susie had died tragically in her teens, and into Susan's relations with all young people, thereafter, went added tenderness.

Of all her devoted corps of younger workers in the movement, Anna Howard Shaw was closest to Susan at the end of her life.

Like Antoinette Brown, Anna Shaw had pioneered in the field of the church. But in Anna's case family opposition had been obdurate and bitter. Penniless and unfriended, she had worked her way through theological school and endured there every variety of petty sex persecution, besides near-starvation and sickness. Something dauntless and stronger than her body had brought her through.

The fires through which Anna passed for her convictions gave her a burning eloquence. She had warmth and magnetism and an Irish wit that captivated her listeners.

Pulpits for women were hard to obtain. It was natural, after the sharp struggles of her youth, that she should be a passionate advocate of women's freedoms. She divided her time between the ministry and the suffrage movement, soon becoming its most gifted speaker.

SIXTEEN

Susan B. Anthony's prestige had reached its height. The influence of her presence at women's congresses, at suffrage conventions and campaigns was now her most important function. At seventy-five Susan was still actively traveling from coast to coast, filling engagements as of old, but more in the capacity of a veteran whose counsel and guidance were invaluable.

She was received reverently wherever she went these days, with touching tributes. On a trip to California hundreds of schoolchildren had marched past her, each one dropping a rose in her lap. On every platform wherever she was to speak, her chair was wreathed in flowers and her arms heaped with fragrance. In San Francisco, audiences stood and cheered. On her way home, city after city staged meetings in her honor.

Describing Susan at a function at this time, the Chicago *Herald* took note of the change the years had wrought.

"Miss Anthony has grown slightly thinner since she was in Chicago attending the World's Fair Congresses, thinner and more spiritual looking. As she sat last night, with her transparent hands grasping the arms of her chair, her thin, hatchet face and white hair, with only her keen eyes flashing light and fire, she looked like Pope Leo XIII. The whole physical being is as nearly submerged as possible in a great mentality."

During the whole of a long life, Susan had become inured to ignominy, slander, ridicule and hatred. Public acclaim was an unaccustomed emotional experience. On top of a prolonged tour of lecturing and travel, this added excitement imposed a great strain on an elderly woman, and strains were something Susan had never had time for.

Shortly after her reception in Chicago, while speaking before the Chautauqua Assembly in Lakeside, Ohio, she ended her address suddenly, groped for her chair, and collapsed.

The press, with its usual enthusiasm for predicting the worst, worked overtime that night. Miss Anthony was not expected to live until morning, read the headlines. However, Susan not only recovered consciousness, but insisted on returning to Rochester next morning.

"If I had pinched myself, real hard," she said disgustedly, "I wouldn't have fainted."

All the hurriedly prepared newspaper obituaries had to be filed away. Susan heard about them later. "Five thousand words if living, no limit if dead," had been the instructions to one Chicago reporter. She had plenty of time to laugh over the affair. A deadly lassitude assailed her after she got home. It was nervous prostration, said her doctor in Rochester. He put her to bed for a month.

But the following year Susan went out West for a bitterly fought election campaign to enfranchise the women of California, and withstood the conflict and the disappointment of defeat as hardily as ever.

Three years later, her International Council of Women, acting now under its own impetus, met in London and desired her presence. For the second time she went abroad.

Who but Susan would have had the calm American effrontery to suggest that Queen Victoria greet this very un-Victorian gathering of women? The result was a reception at Windsor Castle for the entire Congress.

Susan alone was personally introduced. She had not expected to find the sovereign so aged and so infirm. Moved with pity, she took the trembling hand extended to her in her friendly clasp. It was not etiquette, but the half-blind Queen must have felt its sincerity and warmth.

Ever since Elizabeth Cady Stanton's resignation, eight years ago, the burden of the Presidency of the Suffrage Association had fallen upon Susan. Now the movement was expanding its activities very fast and Susan was approaching her eightieth birthday. It was time to "let go," as she herself admitted.

There were two possible candidates for the office: the Reverend Anna Howard Shaw, whose winning personality made her a popular choice, and young Mrs. Carrie Chapman Catt. The latter, while not so colorful, had a genius for planning and a tenacity which could weather years of further struggle, years which Susan foresaw. Miss Shaw felt herself better suited as a lecturer, and although she served as President later, the nomination now fell to Mrs. Catt.

The last convention at which Susan presided convened in Washington, scene of her many battles with Congress, and home of her old Suffrage Association. It was known that this was to be a leave-taking. Reporters jammed the press section and women from all over the country crowded into the capital for the historic occasion.

As Susan sat looking down on the great assembly, on the hundreds of friendly faces upturned to her in pride and affection, her thoughts must have traveled back to the pitiful beginnings of this now vigorous Movement.

A shabby handbag, stuffed with tracts, had once been the sole companion of her weary, discouraged, persistent and undaunted journeyings from door to door. In the midnight stillness of Elizabeth Cady Stanton's house, burning decisions had been made, when the fate of a cause hung on the courageous planning of two wakeful women.

A profound hush settled on the audience as Susan rose to make her farewell address. Of all those in the vast hall, she alone seemed to have command of herself. Even hardboiled members of the press wept unashamedly.

But as Susan said, she was only letting go "of the machinery, not of the spiritual part" of her work. For a long time yet the house in Rochester was to throb with the pulse of her energetic planning, her sudden descents on some local board in defense of local women, the constant click of her typewriter.

On one of her trips to New York City at this time, she stopped off to visit a few days with Elizabeth Cady Stanton who had come to America to await the end. Elizabeth was totally blind now, but still valiant, facing her darkness with a fortitude and gaiety that started the tears in Susan's eyes.

"Shall I see you again?" Susan asked when she left, and there was an inescapable note of fatality in the question.

Elizabeth threw off the implication.

"Yes, if not here, then in the hereafter—if there is one," she countered, adding with her old impish chuckle, "If there isn't, we shall never know it."

Seven months later Elizabeth was gone.

"If I had died first, she would have found beautiful words to describe our friendship," was Susan's pathetic comment when asked to pay tribute to her old friend.

But the thrust of events which she herself had begun left Susan little time for looking backwards. Four states in the Union had enfranchised their women by this time. Everywhere there were active suffrage clubs, working under the direction of a national headquarters.

The winning of the franchise state by state was swelling the number of congressmen willing to support a federal amendment. An annual descent of women on the capital to demand its adoption was never neglected.

In the wake of twentieth-century invention and new machinery, women were being pushed into competitive labor with men, not so much by their own will as by the currents of progress. More and more they felt the sex discrimination in the fields now opening to them. From every class and from every line of endeavor they were joining the suffrage ranks.

In Europe a real awakening, fostered by the activities of the International Council, had begun. In the spring of 1904, Susan was again invited to be the chief guest of the Council, this time in Berlin. She was now eighty-four.

Honored on this occasion by special attention from the

Empress, Susan expressed the hope that the Kaiser, who had raised Germany to economic parity with the United States, would raise German women to a higher place than American women had yet been accorded.

The Empress hesitated a moment, confronted perhaps with her own predicament as wife of a War Lord. "The gentlemen," she reminded Susan at last, with a faintly wry smile, "are very slow to comprehend this movement."

On Susan's return to the United States she continued to be astonishingly active for one of her years. Bodily vigor decreased but her spirit seemed to gain stature. She went indomitably on, never allowing feebleness to interfere with any important obligation.

Those present at the Washington convention which celebrated her eighty-sixth birthday were startled by her frailty. Her message at that meeting was spoken haltingly, out of weakness she strove to hide. It was never forgotten. "Failure is impossible," were her closing words, and the last Susan uttered on any platform. They became the rallying cry of the women who carried on.

Not many weeks later, a brief but severe illness sapped what was left of her strength. She sank into unconsciousness from which she never wakened.

Her passing was mourned the world over. Susan B. Anthony had become an international figure. She had been, also, one of the nation's great soldiers.

She lay in state in the city of Rochester, in a flag-draped coffin. An honor guard of girls, robed in white, stood motionless at her head and feet, keeping silent watch, as thousands of her countrymen filed by.

V

Carrie Chapman Catt

"There is one thing mightier than kings or armies, congresses or political parties—the power of an idea when its time has come to move."

Carrie Chapman Catt,
in her presidential address, 1917

"The rejection this week by the Congress of Honduras of the proposed amendment giving women the right to vote is a discouragement to all those who are working for universal democracy. How can a country claim to be democratic when one-half its citizens are prevented from having any vote in government?"

Editorial in The New York *Times*, March 3, 1952

ONE

About the middle of the eighteenth century, a man named Lane set out for a sparsely settled region north of what is now the New York State border line. With him went a sturdy young wife, a girl built for wilderness living, but too independent, as it turned out, for an average man's comfort.

Like most pioneer wives, Abigail took loneliness, privation and danger in her stride, but the loose morals of frontier life were intolerable and an influence she feared for her children.

Lane was well suited there. As the years passed, his ways grew more shameless and libertine, and in Abigail grew a resolve to return, before it was too late, to the heritage of decency and self-respect she had left.

Between her and home lay a long stretch of wild country and her husband's determination to stay where his vagrant instincts had freer license.

For fifteen years Abigail remained with Lane in the log cabin she had helped him build. At the end of that time she took a hazardous journey alone with her children, through forests and over swamps, rather than continue with him in the life he had chosen.

Her act was one of insubordination. A wife who voluntarily left her husband's roof in those days was harshly judged, no matter what her provocation. Besides the physical risk of her trip, Abigail knew she faced ostracism in a new community.

Several weeks after her departure from the frontier settlement, Abigail walked into a small village in the Adirondacks, leading an oxcart in which were three children. Beside her trudged a tall boy of fifteen and a girl a year younger. Their shoes were roughly made of hide, their clothing of coarse homespun and cured skins. People stared to see a woman travel thus, unaccompanied by a man.

Abigail inquired her way of no one, kept her eye on the road and her head high. She went directly to the house of her brother, a land surveyor, whose home she had left some sixteen years earlier as a bride. Shortly the place buzzed with news of her return. Closemouthed and proud, Abigail gave the gossips little satisfaction and sought no friends.

Whether her brother approved her act of domestic mutiny or no, he gave her shelter. She was stiff-necked, not to be persuaded to go back to Lane. The easiest way out of his predicament was to make his sister self-supporting as soon as possible.

Uncleared land could be claimed without purchase in those days, and a land surveyor knew the best prospects. He built her a home on ground he selected and she and her children aided him.

Abigail managed very well after that. The two oldest children were mature beyond their years with responsibilities she had thrust on them. The work was heavy, too, for a growing girl and boy, but a frontier post had been no fit place for them, and now they could have schooling.

On the land Abigail cleared and planted gradually, generations of Lanes were to come and go. Her property eventually became a part of the city of Potsdam in St. Lawrence County, New York. This pioneer wife who claimed and won her independence in a day when the law gave a dissolute father complete ownership of his children and made a chattel and serf of the mother, became a remote legend to her descendants. To later Lanes, who moved westward on pioneering ventures of their own, her very existence was forgotten, until her qualities reappeared in a great-granddaughter, born in 1859, who dared rebel against wrongs done her sex.

TWO

In the period just before the Civil War, children on lonely Iowa farms learned early to draw on inner resources. Distances between neighbors were great and transportation slow. On the Lane farm, the little girl with the wide-apart blue eyes and active brain was sturdily self-sufficent by the time she was eleven.

Like all farm children, Carrie Lane did her share of the chores, but her hands were never as busy as her mind that pounced eagerly on every printed page within reach. When she had exhausted the few books at home, she read whatever the neighbors would lend her, from religious tracts to farmers' almanacs. Occasionally a volume of poems or a book of ancient history fell into her hands. These treasures she carried to her favorite retreat, a high tree, where she could escape the teasing of a young brother and the commotion of farm life.

The only way to make this borrowed wealth her own was to memorize passages she loved. In her tree she chanted whole poems aloud. Though she did not know it, she was harnessing her tongue to eloquence, a vehicle she was to need some day.

For some time she drifted in this way, down pleasant currents of imagination, but all the time there was a drive and purpose in Carrie which sought expression.

It made her a reformer at twelve. That was the year she discovered the sermons of Robert Ingersoll and had to be restrained from trying to convert the whole neighborhood to a new heresy. But the missionary spirit in her could not be quenched. It shattered her world of dreams one day.

On a solitary errand across her father's meadows one morning, lost in reverie, Carrie was startled by a premonition so strong it seemed like a voice at her elbow.

"There's work for you to do"—how like her mother it spoke —"and you aren't getting ready for it. You've a lot to learn. Stop wasting your time!"

Carrie stood still, thinking intently. They were beginning to call her a dreamer at home, but this was a call from within. She understood dimly that she was standing on a new threshold. Ahead were responsibilities, behind lay childhood. She walked slowly home, resolving on the way to read even more, to study harder and to go to school as long as her father would send her.

There was a presidential election the year Carrie was thirteen. Horace Greeley, Editor of the New York *Tribune,* and General Grant were the candidates. The *Tribune,* containing much political diatribe, arrived daily at the Lane farmhouse, furnishing food for endless debate between her father and the farm hands at mealtime. It was a great deal more fun than the usual talk of pigs and crops.

Carrie, who loved arguments, joined heart and soul in the discussion, asked a thousand questions about "platforms" and "issues," and begged in vain to be allowed to attend campaign rallies with her father and brother. Her budding political ardor was not encouraged by Lucius Lane, puzzled and even embarrassed by his young daughter's interest in matters that were a purely masculine concern.

On Election Day the household was astir early to drive Lucius to the polls. Carrie was surprised to find her mother still placidly at work in the kitchen. Asked if she were not going to change her dress for the trip to town, Mrs. Lane replied calmly that she was staying home.

"But then how can you vote for Greeley?" Carrie demanded in amazement.

The response of the family to that artless question she never forgot. Her brother Charles let out a whoop and rushed to share the joke with the hired man, while her father and mother laughed heartily.

"Voting is only for men—woman's work is in the kitchen," Lucius explained. Carrie set her mouth and marched out of the kitchen deeply humiliated.

While their ridicule was still fresh, a young neighbor called at the house one evening. Supposing he had come to see her brother, Carrie told him where Charles was to be found and left him standing on the doorstep. But it was Carrie he had come to see; the Lane girl, all in one year's time, had become astonishingly pretty. He invited himself in and then fell mute. Equally shy, Carrie searched desperately for a topic of conversation. Her father and mother had gone for a walk. There was no one to help. Finally she launched into the subject still uppermost in her mind.

"My father voted for Greeley. Did yours?"

"Yep."

"It's a national calamity that Greeley wasn't elected." Carrie repeated a remark she'd heard Lucius make.

"Yep."

"If women had been allowed to vote, he'd be President today."

This was certainly no echo of Lucius' opinion and her caller thought it a joke.

"Women vote—" His voice soared high with amusement.

Carrie bristled. "Why shouldn't women vote?"

"It's not lawful." He used the tolerant tone of a boy instructing a girl.

"Men were stupid and unfair to make such a law!"

"What do women know about politics?" he demanded scornfully, starting a violent squabble which only ended when her father and mother appeared. Glad to be rescued, Carrie's visitor fled.

Maria Lane laughed resignedly as she sent Carrie off to bed. "The child hasn't the faintest notion of it, of course, but she's just scared away her first beau."

"Her last, too," Lucius prophesied darkly.

But Lucius was wrong, and Carrie had done better than either of them could guess. She had won her first skirmish in a lifelong crusade.

THREE

Between Lucius and his young daughter there was likewise war, though conducted more amicably. What to do, the
troubled father asked himself, with a girl as different and determined as Carrie? At the rate she was going she'd never find
herself a husband.

Her latest craze was to be a doctor—a female doctor!
Well, he'd better save his breath. She'd be laughed out of
that lunatic idea! Washing his face under the pump, he let
the cold water lower his temperature.

But there was a pressing matter Carrie must settle with
Lucius long before a doctor's career could be even thought
of. The distance to high school was far. Many farmers'
children did not go because no horse could be spared to take
them. When Lucius granted her wish, Carrie proved the
sacrifice worth it by graduating in three years. As for college,
she knew better than to mention it. She took the next steps
herself.

"Who sent you this?" Lucius asked one day, handing her
a college catalogue addressed to *Miss Carrie Lane*.

"I wrote for it."

"Seems queer you wouldn't speak to your mother and me first. How d'you figure I'm going to pay the tuition, if I believed in college for women, which I don't!" Lucius was emphatic.

"I'm going to earn my way, Father."

"*Earn it!*" No daughter of his would hire out to anyone. He'd put his foot down on that!

"I'm going to teach school."

Lucius laughed with relief. "Why, you have to get a certificate to teach first, and before that you have to take an examination."

"I have," said Carrie.

"Suppose you're trying to tell me you're going to teach in the district school here," he suggested with unbelieving sarcasm.

"Yes," said Carrie, "I am."

"Well—I'll be hanged!" Lucius's final remark was addressed to himself.

To Iowa State College Carrie went, entering as a sophomore because she had done the equivalent of a year's work while she taught. Once there, there were ways to meet expenses, like washing dishes at eight cents an hour.

And once there, Carrie unconsciously took the lead in directions which no one else had the spunk or the conviction to explore. Although Iowa State was coeducational, girl students were barred in the 1870's from a number of activities.

On the campus, Carrie had watched the men march in the military drill that was compulsory for a land-grant school. She heard about the physical and mental benefits of the training. Why shouldn't girls be given the same advantages?

"Better not ask for it—the boys will laugh their heads off," advised one of her classmates when she brought the matter up in the pantry after supper.

"Who cares?" retorted Carrie, rinsing out a dishpan with a defiant swish of her cloth. It was not the first challenging question she had put to the dishwashing brigade. They were beginning to be infected with her independence.

"We could drill a sight better than those boys. Most of them can't keep in step. But what about uniforms?" asked someone.

"Percale—blue—" answered Carrie promptly, whipping a pencil from her pocket and drawing on the drain board. "See—we could make them ourselves." They crowded around her, enthusiasm growing.

The matter was soon settled, for Carrie's audacity usually won out with an astounded but amused faculty. "Company G" (for girls) at Iowa State College was the first female troop of its kind. It continued long after Carrie left and foreshadowed the popular WACS and WAVES of today.

At the beginning of her junior year, Carrie accepted the job of assistant college librarian, offered to only a privileged few. During her hours of work there she encountered another honor student whose engineering studies drew him frequently to the library. George Catt, as well as Carrie Lane, had to earn his way. He had no time for the social life of the campus, but Carrie understood that kind of preoccupation. The future was to merge the lives of these two gifted young people, each too intent, for the moment, on reaching a goal.

It did not surprise Carrie's classmates when she was elected to the College Debating Society. It was a top honor few of them envied her, even though she would be allowed merely to read an essay on the chosen subject, since men did the debating and gave the opening oration.

Officers of the Society placed Carrie on the program committee, where they thought a girl might be useful.

"Let's do something that hasn't been done before," Carrie opened fire at the first meeting.

"Fine," agreed the chairman with a trace of condescension. "What's on your mind?"

Carrie produced her innovation with bland composure. "A girl might deliver the oration for a change."

The chairman was the first of the committee to recover.

"Don't know any girl who wouldn't make a fizzle of it," he disagreed flatly, and then catching her slightly ironic smile, he reddened. "Except you," he qualified.

"That's right," the others chimed in, enjoying her discomfort, "the job's yours—you asked for it."

Carrie had yet to learn that a new idea is usually saddled on the initiator. Her counter suggestions were booed down and after some argument she had to admit that no other girl would welcome the honor of breaking this particular precedent. She couldn't back out now without ignominy.

All too soon she found herself on the platform where she had demanded a girl should have the right to sit—in the chair of the orator. The President of the Debating Society made his preliminary remarks and introduced her. Carrie got up like an automaton and walked to the front of the stage.

The agony of her opening sentence once over, others followed in proper sequence. She caught signs of relief in the audience, girls nudged one another triumphantly, members of the faculty nodded approvingly. She was doing better than anyone dared hope. She allowed herself a second's self-congratulation. It was fleeting but it was fatal. In a flash she lost the train of her argument. She began to flounder among words —and then her mind became blank.

She had indeed "made a fizzle of it" and girls would never be allowed to try again! Stricken and humiliated, Carrie turned slowly to leave the stage, when she heard a slight snicker from the men's side of the auditorium. It was all she needed. Her anger blazed and she stepped forward again.

"If you'll give me a minute, I'll be able to go on," she said simply, and that game refusal to quit captured the boys. They broke into applause.

From then on confidence and orderly thinking flowed back. At the end they clapped and shouted till the rafters rang. Carrie hugged to herself two important lessons. A race is never won before the last yard is run and never lost while one chance remains to retrieve a bad start.

FOUR

For a girl in those days, Carrie's career after college was a succession of swift and brilliant advances. Medicine had been an early enthusiasm soon dropped. She wanted to study law now, and took a modest job in a law office near home. A year later, she was asked to become principal of the Mason City High School. The salary was too good to refuse and the work allowed her to go on with her law studies. Then, eighteen months later, at the mature age of twenty-four, she was appointed superintendent of all the Mason City schools.

She inherited from her predecessor in office nine incorrigible young bullies with whom he had been unable to cope and who were terrorizing the schools. The nine soon discovered that the lady superintendent expected obedience and used a strap if she didn't get it. The mutiny was quelled, and those who had thought it insane to put a woman in the job had nothing more to say.

Searching for a local newspaper willing to publish school news written by the students, Carrie one day entered the office of the editor and owner of the Mason City *Republican*, young Leo Chapman. He liked her ideas on education, and after some discussion, became disarmingly confidential about his plans for the future of his paper.

The minutes sped. He forgot that his presses idled and that a new issue of the Mason City *Republican* was due. Miss Lane was a strikingly handsome young woman with sparkling blue eyes and a clear complexion. When Leo finally let her go the stimulation and comradeship of that hour together was unforgettable. Within two weeks, after a gay and impetuous courtship, Carrie was engaged.

It was no part of Leo Chapman's philosophy that a wife should bury her talents in the kitchen. What he offered her was partnership. She was to be assistant editor.

The months which followed were full of happiness for a girl who had known plenty of drudgery on her father's farm, and whose abilities had driven her mercilessly ever since she entered college. It was sheer fun to transform Leo's bare rooms above his office into a comfortable home; to spend evenings sewing up ruffled window curtains while he whistled at his task of making book shelves for the living room, and to show off her skill as a cook.

She and Leo had started a woman's column for their newspaper. Scanning other papers for items of interest for it, Carrie ran across an unobtrusive bit of news one day. A bill to grant municipal suffrage to Iowa women was coming up shortly in the state legislature. She rallied immediately to an old war cry. Had she not, as a child, launched singlehanded in her mother's kitchen a loudly ridiculed campaign for the political equality of women? Now a man was actually sponsoring the idea. Carrie was not one to sit and let others do all the oar-pulling in a boat going her way.

She knew that laws were never passed unless they had plenty of backing. Iowa men were going to be the voters on this question which concerned Iowa women, and toward this particular bill men were more than indifferent—they were antagonistic.

She invited some of the leading women in Mason City to tea. Carrie was not only prominent there now, she was popular. They all accepted, happily ignorant of the arduous work in store for them. The businesslike welcome of their hostess should have warned them, but of business they knew nothing. As each guest took her seat she was handed a paper on which the phrase "We, the undersigned" stood out clearly in Carrie's handwriting. The paper, Carrie explained, was a petition for municipal suffrage. If those present agreed with her on the importance of the suffrage bill, all that remained to be done was to get every woman in Mason City to sign the petition.

"All that remained to be done!" Carrie's guests had imagined they were there to hear her talk on the advantage of voting. Instead they were being asked to do something about it! In the mind of each grew a dismaying picture. Hundreds of women to be called on, to be persuaded to sign a public petition, over the ridicule and protest of their men. The leading ladies of Mason City quailed at the prospect.

"If we divide the work evenly it won't be too hard," Carrie rallied them and prayed for patience. Nothing ever got done, it seemed, without first breaking down mountains of apathy, timidity, prejudice, defeatism! "There are fifteen of us here," she went on, "and we have a month. After we start other women will volunteer."

"Please," came a panicky voice, "I'm no good at talking people into doing something."

"I don't know a thing about politics—"

"I've never made a speech—" others took up the refrain.

"Listen"—Carrie spoke quietly—"you all know a measure is being pushed to sell liquor without license in Iowa. You all know, too, what follows when the controls are off—increased drunkenness, more crime, corruption of youth, prostitution. Whatever undermines society strikes hardest at women and children, and you will never have any say about it until you can vote. What of your sons, if that bill passes?"

The room had grown very still. They were all mothers there. When the vote was related to family problems it became a clear issue.

"This petition of ours," continued Carrie, "isn't likely to win us municipal suffrage. All it will do is show the legislators that women in Mason have waked up, that they demand the right to say 'Yes' or 'No' on issues that affect them. It's a first step, but an important one."

A woman in the room who had four boys was the first to volunteer and the others rapidly followed suit. In a week Carrie had quite an army marshaled to canvass the city. Going with many of them, to show them how to present the matter and win support, she took over the lion's share of the work. When the campaign was ended, the results startled the petitioners themselves as well as the legislators; all but a dozen women in the city had signed.

The petition did not get them the vote but it roused everyone, including the Iowa State Woman Suffrage Association, blazing a slow path through apathy and opposition. They invited Carrie to their state convention at Cedar Rapids. How, they wanted to know, had she produced so many vote-minded women?

Carrie went, only to be disillusioned. The meeting was incredibly dull and spiritless, until a small, gentle-faced old lady in a lace cap rose to her feet. When she heard the famous, silver-toned voice, Carrie recognized Lucy Stone. She did not return to Mason City until she had sat humbly at Lucy's feet drinking in the early history of the feminist movement. As the tale unfolded from the unresentful lips of an aged leader who had been greatly persecuted for her convictions, Carrie saw how rough the road of reformers can be. The story moved her, but she was wedded to Leo at the time, not to a Cause. She could not guess how soon matters would be reversed.

Not many weeks later she was back on the farm with her parents, waiting word from Leo to join him in San Francisco. He had sold his newspaper. They were both agreed that in the West were greater opportunities.

"It seems confoundedly stupid to leave you here," objected Leo too late, as they stood together on the station platform. "I've a good mind to put you on the train just as you are."

But the train had begun to move and there had hardly been time to say good-by. Long afterwards Carrie was to remember the haste and stricken regret of their last embrace.

When a message did come from San Francisco it was signed by an aunt living there. "Come at once. Leo has typhoid," it said. A few days later, on the train carrying her West, a second telegram announced his death. Heartbreak and the shattering of all their youthful hopes and plans were her bitter companions the rest of that tragic journey.

FIVE

Carrie stayed on in San Francisco with the aunt who welcomed her into her home. The way back to usefulness was perplexing and difficult. The shock of Leo's death had robbed her of old interests. Deciding at last to pick up her life where it had broken off, she found a position on a commercial newspaper. Because of her previous experience on a newspaper she was given a fair salary and promise of advancement before long.

But Carrie was much more fortunate than most women forced to earn a livelihood in those days, who worked for pitifully small pay and no chance of betterment. Injustices in the teaching profession she had known. Now she saw the plight of women in business and shared it. Starvation pay was only a part of the picture. Sex was a constant handicap. The attitude of men to women in business was flippant, disrespectful and often offensive.

One afternoon, after hours, her employer asked her to go on an errand to another office. The man in charge there took advantage of the empty rooms to throw his arms around her. Carrie turned on him with such withering scorn that he showed her out with elaborate apologies. She walked home disgusted and almost defeated.

She had learned much during her months in business. Women would never win respect and equal treatment in a field dominated by men unless they matured, claimed their rights and proved their abilities. They needed teaching, training, leadership. How were they to get it?

All at once she saw clearly where events and her own instincts had been leading her all these years. Here at last was her purpose—her mission in life—to open doors unjustly closed to women. Had she not been conscious, even in childhood, of some great work that waited her doing?

Carrie took her next step without hesitation. She resigned from her newspaper job, although how she was to support herself was not yet clear. She was as incapable of half-measures as Lucretia Mott, Elizabeth Cady Stanton, Lucy Stone, and Susan B. Anthony, of whom at this moment she knew little. It was her own inner conviction that impelled her, as reckless of consequences as that of her great predecessors. A few dollars laid aside was all she had to start on.

But before she left San Francisco an unexpected meeting occurred. A passer-by on the street, one day, turned to look at her, then held out his hand.

"Carrie Lane!" he exclaimed. "I thought I couldn't be mistaken!"

It was George Catt, the young engineer who had spent so many hours in the Iowa State College library.

"I suppose," answered Carrie, "you've built all those bridges you used to plot so carefully. I want to hear about them."

But it was she who talked most, drawn by his grave sympathy to speak of the tragedy which had left her stranded in San Francisco. When she told him of her determination to crusade for women, she caught the quick gleam of approval in his eyes. Before George Catt's work called him elsewhere they saw a good deal of each other. When he left he said with one of his rare smiles:

"I was a feminist before you knew the meaning of the word, Carrie. Let me know if there's anything I can do."

SIX

Carrie did not immediately join the suffrage forces—those earnest but rather ineffectual small groups sparsely dotting the country at the time. The meeting she had attended in Cedar Rapids had not impressed her. She wanted to explore the field for herself.

Lecturers still attracted large audiences in the Middle West, so before leaving California and the hospitality of her aunt's home there, Carrie prepared a number of talks on *Great Women in History*. A series of lectures, she knew, would both earn her a living and enable her to start her mission. Women, generally timid and unschooled, must be made aware of their heritage.

Her new work started in Iowa. Country women there showed great eagerness for the world she described that lay beyond their kitchen walls. But there were always exceptions, she found.

Mrs. Jones, who never missed a church social and could remember down to the last hook and whalebone what each woman wore, agreed with Mrs. Brown that a young, good-looking widow like Carrie Chapman was inviting too much attention with her public talks—especially on so questionable a theme as emancipated woman!

"She don't look broken, not a mite," she complained. "Now my health was poorly for five years after John died."

"College does it—it hardens women," lamented Mrs. Brown. "I'm glad my Ethel never caught the craze. She's a devoted wife and mother."

Local clergymen challenged Carrie on doctrinal grounds. Why offer Zenobia, a heathen queen, to Christian women as a model? Didn't Paul preach that women must be submissive to their husbands—and silent in public? they added pointedly.

Carrie thanked them for the reminder and produced the Biblical characters Deborah and Esther. One had led a successful campaign against the Canaanites and the other had outwitted a crafty politician. Routed on their own ground the clergymen subsided, but never gracefully.

Churches were the only available meeting-places in most Midwest towns and clergymen usually officiated. They seldom failed to take advantage of their privilege.

"O, Lord," one minister opened a meeting of Carrie's, "we are met together to hear a young woman make a speech. Enable us to disbelieve what she says contrary to the Scriptures. Help us remember that woman was from the beginning the serpent's mouthpiece, and caused the fall of man." At the end of her lecture he rose again. "Good Lord," he paused with raised hand to let his words sink in, "lay what this woman hath said aside—forget it!"

But her listeners never forgot it. As the clergy feared, they went away imbued with the dangerous doctrine that woman's sphere had suddenly expanded.

News of her successful lectures reached the Iowa State Suffrage Association. Young Mrs. Chapman, once famous for her activities in Mason City, was awakening women all over the state to take an interest in their local government, and attracting a large following. The Association desperately needed a following too. Would she, they asked, head their campaign for more members?

Carrie hesitated. She had to earn her living. The work asked of her was time-consuming and unpaid. In the end she shouldered it, though it meant less lecturing and more frugal living. Like those before her who had worn patched clothes and sacrificed all comforts to further an unpopular cause, she was never to count the cost of her effort nor take a cent in return for her labors in behalf of women.

With all her lectures she now managed to include a talk on the structure of government. Carrie had noticed, from the blank expressions on the faces of her audiences, that few understood the terms she used. A naïve voice once inquired:

"The White House is the President's home, but who lives in the House of Representatives?"

Then and there Carrie offered to draw them a diagram showing the different departments of government. They brought the blackboard up from the Sunday school and had their first lesson. Out of that experience grew the pamphlet she wrote describing state and federal institutions. Later, it became part of official suffrage literature, distributed all over the country.

Meanwhile, three years had elapsed since her meeting in California with George Catt. His letters told very little of the prominence he was attaining as an engineer. They were full of a matter more important to him. "Marry me—and see what a team we'll make," he pleaded much as Henry Blackwell had pleaded with Lucy Stone. "I'm earning a great deal too much for one. Let me make a living for us both and you will have more time and energy for the Movement."

But Carrie couldn't see it. "It would be unfair to you. I'm giving all I have to this crusade—there'd be nothing left for you."

So she struggled on alone, finding it more and more difficult to make ends meet while she devoted time to the unpaid work which seemed so vital. For Carrie had come to the decision that lecturing on women's past achievements was not the answer. Talk would never advance them nor change unjust laws. Her goal had become the winning of the franchise.

SEVEN

Soon after that decision, she went as a modest young delegate from Iowa to the memorable meeting in 1890 in Washington which merged the two opposing suffrage parties into one Association. It was her first big convention and she was scheduled to make a brief speech.

By now, Carrie had heard of the disagreement between Susan B. Anthony's followers and those of Lucy Stone. She was immensely curious to see these first champions of woman's rights. Obstinacy had been their strongest weapon and diehards don't change overnight. Could these spirited pioneers really reconcile their differences?

As the delegates began to assemble, Susan B. Anthony was easily recognizable, the most dominant figure there for all her seventy years. Her classic Roman features were matched in dignity by her plain black dress. Her one adornment, the famous crimson shawl, hung over one arm, flashing its defiance as of old.

"I see you don't know them all," a kindly woman in the next seat whispered to Carrie. "That portly woman wearing the rich black mantilla over her white hair—yes, the lively one at Miss Anthony's left—is Elizabeth Cady Stanton, the most brilliant of the old guard and the most irrepressible."

Carrie watched the two celebrities deep in talk, the one full of exuberant spirits, the other Spartan in her strength. She had never seen a more revealing contrast.

Carrie almost forgot her part in the meeting as the pioneer leaders spoke in turn. It was not only the legendary quality of their names that held her spellbound. There was a glint in their eyes, a drive and power in their delivery that she missed in speakers of her own generation. Only Anna Howard Shaw, a brilliant young newcomer to the Movement and Miss Anthony's favorite, had an equal fire.

In recognition of her position as the earliest living pioneer, Elizabeth Cady Stanton was elected President of the newly formed Association. Her speech of acceptance indicated that her views had lost none of their punch, just because she was now joined to advocates of appeasement. With a wicked twinkle, she urged the assembly not to "fear the opinion of others," nor be "silent from motives of policy."

When at last her time came to speak, Carrie felt very much a novice. It was these earlier crusaders who had borne the full violence of persecution. What had she to tell them, beyond the assurance that the standard of woman's rights would be seized by hands as consecrated as their own?

But that, after all, was what they wanted most to hear.

Carrie's rich young voice reached easily to the farthest rows. Even at this early stage her poise—a sense of mastery in her whole bearing, was striking. In Susan's eyes a spark of recognition flared. This was the stuff of which a leader could be made. She wished there were hundreds like her.

Carrie's presence in Washington sealed her affiliation with the Suffrage Movement. Before the meeting was over she had volunteered to serve in her first suffrage campaign under Miss Anthony. Before embarking on it, however, she had time to fulfill a promise made to George Catt, whose suit had persisted in spite of everything. They were married in Seattle, where he was in charge of important railroad construction. The first two months of married life set the pattern for their future, for George Catt was as wedded to his engineering as she was to a cause.

He could not leave the immense project he directed, so Carrie frequently went with him to the scene of action. Watching him handle an enterprise involving vast sums and immense numbers of men, seeing him make instant decisions in emergencies, she was able to estimate the caliber of the man she had married. It was a lesson in organization she never forgot, and, for her at least, it was a period of complete freedom, the first she had known in all her thirty-one years.

Immediately after this brief honeymoon, Carrie joined Miss Anthony's campaign in South Dakota. There she saw the suffrage issue collide with one of the most powerful of its opponents—the liquor interests. It was election time, and frantic efforts were being made to repeal a recently passed state prohibition law. Aware that women were a solid bloc in favor of temperance, South Dakota wets were working for their defeat and using all the tricks known to a wily and lawless foe.

At the political rallies all over the state, attended by suffrage delegates, their opponents saw to it that the women were seated in the rear of the halls and crowded off the programs. Everything was done to insult and humiliate these newcomers to a political arena which had always belonged to men.

In the city of Pierre, a delegation of Sioux braves in full regalia was escorted to the best seats with a flourish of trumpets. Each brave wore a large badge on which was printed in big letters: "Against Woman Suffrage and Susan B. Anthony." As they couldn't read, they hadn't the faintest notion what the caption meant. The same trick was played in Aberdeen with another group of illiterates, Russian immigrants.

Meanwhile, Miss Anthony sent suffrage speakers through the rural districts of South Dakota, bringing to lonely homesteaders the news of a move to advance women, explaining the need to become full-fledged citizens and describing the uses of the ballot.

Quite frankly, Miss Anthony allotted to Carrie the poorest and least promising sections to stump. "I wouldn't ordinarily send a woman alone on this assignment, but we're terribly shorthanded and you have the stamina. It will take all you have," warned the older woman, her searching gray eyes taking the measure of her new recruit.

So Carrie went off, greatly bolstered by her chief's confidence. She was used to fertile areas in Iowa where farmers made a comfortable living. South Dakota that year was a parched and arid land, scorched by five years of drought.

Her first talk was given in a grain elevator to an audience of fifteen. The women's faces under their faded sunbonnets were listless and hollow-eyed, the men's bony frames sagged in loose garments. They had driven horses as jaded as themselves miles, just to look at a stranger and hear something new. It seemed to Carrie an impertinence to bring an abstract idea like woman suffrage to people who were obviously starving.

Yet they had come because they wanted to. Familiar with the mentality of farm women, she reduced the subject to simple, practical terms and showed them how the power of the vote could lift them out of degrading conditions, improve their communities and build a future for their children. Here and there she detected intense interest in some unstirring figure, caught an answering gleam in dull eyes.

When she ended, they filed out into the night as wearily and inscrutably as they had walked in, asking no questions. Carrie felt she must have failed.

"Somehow—I didn't reach your friends," she said dejectedly to the local postmaster who had sponsored the meeting.

"Pshaw! They never says much. Talk here got dried up with the crops. A diet of watermelon wouldn't pep up a fly—you did right well," he consoled her.

Several weeks of campaigning taught Carrie just what he meant. In the rude cabins in which she stayed, watermelon and bread was the only food. But they shared what they had, gladly, and Carrie no longer felt apologetic for her mission. Women might be starved, but they crowded the granaries and schoolhouses where she spoke, bringing children with them who couldn't be left behind. Seeing them rock the smallest in their tired arms, Carrie suggested pooling them all in the center of the floor on blankets, where they slept happily through the evening.

To bring these unhappy, burdened women some hint of opportunity, she saw, was like bringing water to their parched crops. She was opening a door for them which would never shut completely again.

Woman Suffrage was not won in South Dakota that year, nor was it won in most of the various states in which Carrie campaigned during the next ten years. It became plain to her that to be successful, a campaign must be prepared months in advance. The active backing of local citizens and political groups was essential. Ample funds must be collected to pay the expenses of speakers and delegates, and a far greater number of volunteer suffrage workers must be enlisted and trained.

EIGHT

Meanwhile Miss Anthony found she had not overestimated the abilities of the young woman from Iowa, who through her recent marriage had become Carrie Chapman Catt.

Though still an apprentice she was one of the few chosen by Miss Anthony to speak at the annual hearing granted suffragists by the Judiciary Committee of the House of Representatives.

With her first appearance before members of Congress, Carrie's somewhat awed respect for the nation's legislators suffered a speedy eclipse. Members of the Committee yawned insultingly or slept through the women's speeches. To Miss Anthony, the indifference of Congress was too old a story to get excited about.

"Some day they'll have to listen to us," she answered Carrie's indignation. "Save your energies to speed that day."

But Carrie thought privately that suffragists had invited some of that indifference. "We women didn't make too good a showing," she decided. "None of us knew what points the others would cover. They told me I would come last—and then they called on me to make the opening speech. Naturally,

I wasn't prepared. Next year we must plan carefully and not duplicate our efforts."

Much later, under Carrie's leadership, these annual hearings in Washington were staged with an attention to detail which caused her subordinates many a headache and gave Congress something to think about.

Soon after this, on her own initiative, Carrie organized a conference covering the entire Mississippi Valley. National leaders of the Movement were asked as guest speakers. Miss Anthony, somewhat taken aback that she had not been consulted on so important a matter, arrived in some agitation, only to be reassured by what she saw.

Keen, alert young women crowded the conference hall. The atmosphere was filled with vitality and a buoyancy unknown to an earlier generation. A life-giving current was flowing into the suffrage movement here in the Middle West, and with it a flow of money into the treasury. At the conference, Carrie presented to the Mississippi workers the same plan for financing and membership she had devised for the Iowa field. Miss Anthony saw its worth immediately.

"If this is what you can do, you'll have to be Finance Chairman for the National Association. Oh, I know," she laughed, seeing the younger woman's dismay, "but people with ideas are always headed for responsibility."

Carrie's only answer was the wry little smile with which she was beginning to accept life's contradictions. She had pledged herself to help women, at whatever cost. The demands of the movement were increasing, robbing her of the rich companionship she was finding in her second marriage, forcing her to break the contract she had made with George Catt for a specified amount of free time. But George, used to huge business projects that expanded constantly, was more prepared than she for what was happening.

"If you'd been in this crusade as long as I have," he rallied her with his old joke, "you'd be used to the pace."

It was fortunate he took so philosophical a view, for by now Carrie's reputation for getting things done was drawing her into every major effort.

The women of Colorado had sent an urgent plea to Miss Anthony. They were about to launch a suffrage campaign and the prospects were favorable. If one of the celebrated pioneers could be persuaded to enlist, its success, they claimed, would be assured. But Lucy Stone was already stricken with her last illness, and Miss Anthony was engaged to campaign elsewhere. It was left to Carrie to step into the breach.

When she reached Colorado, she found the area given her held the toughest elements of the Rocky Mountain mining camps. As usual, she was handed the job everyone else dreaded.

Few women braved the Colorado mining districts. The prospectors stormed the halls where she spoke. Boisterous horseplay and a powerful aroma of alcohol blew in with them. How to make a woman's cause appeal to these hard-bitten adventurers would have baffled the most seasoned speaker.

To Carrie's surprise they listened attentively, quick to grasp that hers was a plea for equality and justice. Some were fugitives from the law, most of them remembered better days, and all of them were disillusioned. They treated her with a respect that was as touching as it was unexpected.

"Lady," a huge-limbed Irishman shuffled up to her after one

lecture, "I'm what they call a bad man—drunk, or in jail most of the time. It's your kind should balance off the likes of me. I'm for woman suffrage!"

The early pioneers of woman's rights had established a proud tradition. They allowed nothing to stand in their way. Carrie's tour through the Rockies enabled her to emulate them. A bad train wreck once blocked her route to Durango, where she was scheduled to speak that evening.

The operator of a small, single-track road offered her a push-car, provided someone could be found to operate it as far as the wreck.

Once there, the wreckers might be persuaded to take her to Durango.

"It's a seventy-mile coast, but if the lady's game for the ride, I'll take her," drawled a veteran rounder. He had only one arm.

By the time Carrie discovered what a push-car was—a wooden platform on wheels and without brakes—most of the town had collected to see her off, and there was nothing to do but swallow her consternation. In guileless ignorance of what was coming, she accepted the loan of an extra hatpin. Someone placed a bag of sandwiches in her lap, the crowd gave a shove, and the push-car moved off at a comfortable pace.

Perched in front, her feet braced against a rope, both hands clutching the edge, Carrie decided with relief that her fears were unfounded. But the car gathered momentum down a long slope. After that, she hung on for dear life, as she and her companion rocketed through canyons and over mountain streams at breakneck speed. Her hat blew off, the sandwiches soared after it and Carrie wondered grimly why she hadn't insisted on an able-bodied operator. That one-armed man had been pitched off rounding the last corner, no doubt.

Relief was intense when the smell of scorched wood told her he was applying a board to the wheels, an improvised brake which slowed them not a whit. By some miracle she and the rounder were still intact when the push-car rolled to a gradual stop on an upgrade in front of the wrecking train.

When she reached Durango that night, she spoke to a waiting audience without having had time to eat. After midnight she got a meal and two hours' sleep before leaving for her next destination. To a campaigner for the woman's crusade it was all in the day's work. Colorado was the second state to write woman suffrage into its constitution, and Carrie was credited with having made a major contribution to victory.

NINE

In other parts of the country, however, the liquor and vice industries, fearing a huge decline in trade once women were empowered to vote, arrayed themselves against the suffrage forces and defeated them. Big business, profiting enormously from child labor and underpaid female workers, likewise opposed woman suffrage.

These three vested interests combined to oppose women, bribing or coercing voters, politicians and election officers wherever the suffrage issue came up. Woman suffrage occasionally won a majority in state legislatures, but it was always defeated in the people's elections by dishonest balloting. Fraudulent counts were made and ballot boxes "stuffed" with illegally cast votes. Years passed before women detected all the trickery and intrigue employed. Gradually they developed a strategy of their own.

Part of that strategy was to carry the fight into every state in the Union. The South, the most conservative and reactionary area in the country, had never been penetrated. Steeped in a romantic tradition, women themselves offered the most effective opposition. They belonged to a sisterhood which eventually organized themselves into the "what-do-women-want-that-they-haven't-already-got?" group, known more briefly as antisuffragists.

Yielding to the new policies of a younger generation of followers whom she affectionately dubbed her "cabinet," Miss Anthony was persuaded to tour the deep South alone with Carrie. The veteran leader's name, once so abused, commanded respect even there, and drew audiences that came out of curiosity, if for no other reason. But for Carrie, burdened with the entire management of the trip and most of the speaking, traveling with an aged leader was like being made responsible for a fragile and very valuable exhibit.

Miss Anthony's memory had become capricious. Sometimes she held the floor for half an hour. More often she spoke only five minutes, when it was Carrie's business to pick up the thread of argument where her chief had dropped it, weaving it into her own speech in such a way that no break was apparent.

The apathy of Southerners was difficult to pierce and ten times more exhausting than the challenge of hostile audiences. After her meetings, Carrie frequently went for a solitary walk to wear off her discouragement.

Coming back to her lodgings one night when matters had gone worse than usual, she found that unquenchable warrior, Miss Anthony, reading placidly in bed. Her back was propped with ramrod straightness against the pillows, a crocheted shawl covered her Mother Hubbard nightdress and goldrimmed spectacles bridged her judicial nose.

"Well?" Miss Anthony looked up from her book, mildly surprised at her aide's distraught expression.

"My speech," faltered Carrie, "I never made a worse one." The old leader peered at Carrie over her glasses, eyes full of cynical amusement.

"Gracious, is that all? I've made plenty, and the cause has survived, as you see. Get some sleep, child. You'll feel all right tomorrow. It's a hundred times better to make a poor speech for suffrage than none at all."

And so it proved. In every Southern state they visited, a few passionate believers were found who now became enthusiastic workers. Carrie started Suffrage Clubs in almost all the towns where she and Miss Anthony spoke. Most important of all she appointed delegates to the forthcoming National Convention, held that year in Atlanta, Georgia. For the first time in Suffrage history, women of the South joined the crusade.

At this Atlanta Convention, Carrie was elected Chairman of Organization for the entire Field. Although many brilliant women were holding positions of prominence in the Movement by this time, planning on a broad scale was Carrie's special gift and she had a genius for stirring people to action.

Her program for the coming year, presented at the convention, warned the delegates that they were entering a new phase in the suffrage fight. Bluntly she laid before the assembly the slight gains of the Movement in the last forty years. A few outstanding leaders had labored heroically for the Cause. Now women must win their freedom as every other group had, by concerted effort.

The silence in the auditorium as she spoke bristled with challenges. Leaders of branch associations had enjoyed, up to now, great independence of action—with sometimes disastrous results. They had never been bothered by suggestions from "Headquarters."

"The National Association chronically lacks funds." Carrie aimed this indisputable fact at the sour faces she saw spotting the hall here and there. Miss Anthony's dry chuckle was audible, and a murmured "Hear, hear!" from the front seats.

"We must appoint organizers," Carrie went on, "plenty of them. They must travel from coast to coast, forming suffrage societies and raising funds for the National Association.

"We should stage four regional conferences a year, in the North, South, West and the East, to report progress and iron out sectional difficulties. Suffrage Clubs have become mere social centers. Why shouldn't they hold classes in parliamentary law and teach the fundamentals of government? I propose that the National Association print and distribute a syllabus of instruction."

As Carrie's low voice continued to list suggestions, there was a hushed stir in the audience. She was opening up channels for limitless, positively terrifying activity. The applause when she finally sat down was restrained.

"The weak and tired amongst us had better read the handwriting on the wall," one woman chuckled to her neighbor.

Miss Anthony herself was slightly jolted by Carrie's unflattering survey of the Movement's accomplishments to date. Each new generation was sure matters would have progressed faster had they been at the helm, she remarked somewhat ironically in her closing address.

The little dig was not lost on Carrie, who had no delusions about the joys of leadership. She had stepped into its glare and must expect to become a target.

Back at Bensonhurst, a suburb of Brooklyn, where she and George Catt had established a home, the Chairman of Organization plunged into the program of work she had herself initiated. Used to labor that would have floored an average person, Carrie supposed she could tackle it singlehanded. Perhaps she might have, but unexpected emergencies always arise.

It was suddenly imperative to launch an energetic campaign in South Carolina, where the state constitution was being revised. At a time like that, legislators might be induced to include woman suffrage.

The whole Missouri Suffrage Association had collapsed. She must find someone capable of picking it up and setting it in motion again.

Meantime, that syllabus of instruction she had so glibly proposed awaited her writing. Files, stationery, printed pamphlets, innumerable memoranda and notes littered the library at Bensonhurst. Carrie's correspondence alone could have kept two people busy. She finally engaged a stenographer and sent an SOS to the secretary of her committee to come and help.

TEN

The end of that five-year period marked the beginning of a new era. Miss Anthony, the only surviving pioneer, resigned her leadership of the Movement. She was to nominate her successor, and it was known her choice lay between two women. The Reverend Anna Howard Shaw was like a daughter to Miss Anthony. With other women who pioneered in the ministry, she had braved every sort of persecution. Adored for her ready wit and the high drama of her oratory she invariably attracted immense audiences. So magnetic and stirring a personality could be invaluable at the head of a still-ridiculed crusade.

But the Cause was something more than a crusade now. It was a far-flung organization, needing the executive skills and political sagacity of Carrie Chapman Catt. Hers would be leadership of a different kind, emphasizing the training of great numbers of efficient suffrage workers and demanding of them the same selfless devotion to an idea which she herself gave. Besides—who else was as free to donate all her time to the Movement?

Carrie accepted the promotion with deep reluctance. She

knew others had aspired to the office, and that any successor to so eminent a figure as Miss Anthony must suffer by comparison. Her whole life had been subordinated to the Cause. It needed only this last call to cap the climax of pressures.

Consulting her husband, she found he would never cry halt in his own interests. Pointing out to Carrie that she had for some time been the actual guiding force behind the aging Miss Anthony, he asked how the Presidency could be much more demanding? Spurred by his calm acceptance of her role, Carrie finally consented.

Miss Anthony's resignation took place at the annual meeting of the National Association in Washington. Facing the solemn conclave gathered to pay tribute to a beloved and venerated leader, Carrie shared the wave of emotion that swept the assembly. Regret that the old order had come to an end was overpowering. It cast its inevitable shadow on the new President, and on the welcome due her.

Miss Anthony made her farewell speech. Then, in the tense hush, she led Carrie to the front of the stage. The younger woman stood silent a moment, struggling with a crushing sense of loneliness. Unless the Field was willing to sink petty differences and jealousies in a common effort, she would face tragic failure.

Her speech was brief. There could be no "leader" after Miss Anthony, Carrie said. She would merely serve as every other officer of the Association did. She stressed the impossibility of her task unless they all pulled together. Her few words went far toward disarming what resentment may have lurked that a favorite had not been selected.

Carrie was little aware of her effect upon others, but as

she unwillingly stepped now into a position of great prominence, the newspapers were not slow to perceive the fitness of Miss Anthony's choice.

Like most people much before the public, Carrie had developed and perfected a stage presence which added immensely to the prestige of the Cause she served. The Boston *Globe* described her as towering easily above other speakers.

"Hers is finished speech," said the newspaper. "There isn't much left to talk about when she gets through. There is never a slip of the tongue, no hesitancy, and her arguments are piled one on another like the charge of a judge to the jury. The effect is irresistible."

Her appearance on a platform was striking. Carrie was very handsome, always impeccably gowned in the shades of blue that became her so well. She had acquired a suave and unshakable poise, but her retort could be swift and merciless, as people who baited her soon learned.

Yet behind the head of the Movement, behind the tireless brain that planned indefatigably and brilliantly for the Cause, was a plainswoman, simple, unassuming and forthright, bred on the soil and proud of her heritage—the daughter of Iowa farmers.

No one but George Catt knew how often she thought of the family and the farm back in Iowa. Only he knew how anxious she was for Lucius, beginning to admit his failing health, for her mother, fast becoming an invalid, and a favorite young brother who was fighting a dangerous disease.

At home, she watched her husband take on mountainous responsibilities as his engineering company became a leading concern. The strain on his health was beginning to show. Anxious on his account, Carrie felt a vacation was imperative. Her suffrage activities had already been interrupted by a painful difficulty of her own, but it seemed impossible to stop unless someone else needed a rest.

The European trip which she and George Catt embarked on in the summer of 1903 was the first real relaxation they had ever allowed themselves. Now, in their mid-forties, the pace was broken at last, not to be resumed—while they were together—with quite the same intensity. Their journey was a rediscovery of themselves. George Catt feasted his eyes on architectural marvels he had dreamed of seeing when he was a struggling young engineer. Carrie felt a thirst revive in her, forgotten since she had chanted poetry as a child.

Back in harness again in the States, the good effects of their trip wore off too quickly. Her husband returned to work as stubbornly as do most successful people whose projects are important to them. He came back from his office at the end of each day fagged out. To Carrie he seemed to be aging under her eyes. If she couldn't persuade him to slow down, she could at least take on less work herself.

She resigned from the Presidency, because the demands of the office necessitated long absences from home. To the officers of the National Association, aghast at her withdrawal and using every persuasion they could think of, she said flatly and finally: "My husband needs me. All I have done for the suffrage cause I have been able to do by his generosity. I will not leave him."

Anna Howard Shaw now took up the burden of heading the Movement. The spade work done by Carrie had set the pattern of suffrage campaigns for years to come. Miss Shaw, who had far less time to give the Movement, was thus able to leave a great deal to competent aides, and concentrate on those abilities which were her special gift.

For Carrie there remained plenty of suffrage work at home. The following summer, George Catt had business abroad. Carrie attended the International Council of Women with Miss Anthony in Berlin, and joined him in England afterwards. Once more they had a period of leisure together, touring the British Isles.

When autumn came and they were settled again in New York, her husband looked rested and Carrie dared hope he was learning to interrupt work and relax. The end came entirely without warning. George Catt was stricken suddenly in his office. He lingered only a few weeks, and then Carrie was left alone with memories of a devoted companion, who had supported her unfailingly as he had promised. It was to be a year of tragic loss. Within the next few months Miss Anthony died, and Carrie lost her mother and the young brother who had been specially close to her.

Fortunately, there would always be work to mitigate her loneliness. But the home she had shared with her husband was now unbearably empty. She moved into another in New York City, and Mary Garrett Hay, long associated with her in suffrage work, came to live with her. The two friends remained together until Miss Hay's death.

ELEVEN

To trace Carrie's emergence from this point to the international figure she became, is to follow the spread of the Woman's Crusade as it gradually circled the globe. George Catt had left his widow with ample means. During their travels they had both been struck by the unhappy lot of women in countries where feudal laws and customs still predominated.

She felt she could devise no better memorial to him than to use his wealth to help bring some measure of freedom to these retarded women.

Before Miss Anthony died, she had joined enthusiastically in Carrie's project for an International Woman Suffrage Alliance. It was still an infant organization, needing leadership to develop into a world influence. Carrie devoted all her time to it now, and enlisted the aid of the most gifted women in Europe. She inaugurated a series of World Conferences, to convene every two years. Copenhagen, Amsterdam, London, Stockholm, Budapest in turn opened their doors to huge congresses of women.

Delegates from all parts of the world brought moving evidence of the longing of their compatriots for greater freedom. One such proof was a petition sent by a group of illiterate Russian women to the newly created Russian Parliament:

"We peasant women of Tver," it read, "are told that the Duma can change the law. Then tell the Duma that all must be admitted to the Duma, rich and poor, men and women. Otherwise there will be no peace in family life. Formerly, we had the same rulers as our husbands. Now we hear that our husbands are going to write the rules for us. This is unjust, it is an offense to women. They do not understand what we want.

"We are uneducated and beg to be forgiven if we have not written well. We do not write our names for fear of our husbands and our rulers."

United on the subject of woman's rights, members of the Alliance sometimes forgot that war was not a safe subject to introduce.

"If German women had had the vote during our dispute with Germany over Schleswig-Holstein, the German army would never have dared commit so many atrocities in our conquered provinces," was the happy comment made by one Danish delegate. Whereupon all the German members of the Alliance walked out and were induced to return only by the utmost persuasion.

It was plain the Alliance must further international accord as well as woman's advance. In her addresses before these immense gatherings, Carrie called on her listeners to bury their national antagonisms and pride and work for the entire family of man.

The year the London Congress met, English suffragists, led by Emmeline Pankhurst, were in the midst of a sensational fight for their rights. It was viewed with mixed reactions by the visitors. As President of the Alliance, Carrie was urged to make some official statement, either of condemnation or support of the British militants.

"I have no intention of condemning or upholding militant tactics," she replied in her opening address, "but I also have no intention of evading the issue. As an international body, we must not take sides in a contention over methods in a single country. You and I, delegates to this convention, if we are courteous, diplomatic, just—if we understand what internationalism really means—will be silent upon our opinions concerning that issue."

When Emmeline Pankhurst was released from jail, Carrie wrote a friend: "I glory in the fight and spunk of these women." Nevertheless, the breaking of windows and other acts of violence, to force granting of the franchise, were in her opinion more harmful to the Cause than otherwise. In America, the processes of education had already worked a great change in the status of women.

Until World War I made it impossible for the International Alliance to function, Carrie worked incessantly to improve the condition of foreign women. China, Japan, India, Malaya, Dutch East Indies, the Philippines, North Africa, Argentina, Brazil were only some of the countries she visited on this mission. The ten years in which she headed the Alliance gave a tremendous impetus to woman's rights all over the world.

By 1914, twelve states in Carrie's own country had adopted woman suffrage. By this time, also, Americans were accustomed to women in business. They were no longer shocked when they saw a woman enter a bank unescorted by a man, to transact her affairs. They accepted women on public platforms and grudgingly admitted them to the professions. The American woman had come a long way since the year 1840, when Margaret Fuller caused a near riot in Boston by sitting down in a public library to read.

From now on, as the fight for the Federal Amendment speeded up, men were to see their wives and daughters mount soapboxes on the streets to harangue passers-by on the issue of votes for women. News of suffrage activities were on the front page of almost every newspaper. All the major cities were treated to the spectacle of great suffrage parades, in which marched women from every walk of life, from factory girls to eminent leaders in the professions and the arts. The eyes and ears of the public were being constantly bombarded with evidence that, in spite of contrary assertions from anti-suffragists, American women were clamoring for the vote.

Government Representatives in states where suffrage had been granted had now to reckon women among their constituents. If they wanted to remain in office, they dared not oppose woman suffrage in Congress. Very slowly but certainly, the tide was turning.

Meantime the war had virtually dissolved the International Alliance. Carrie was now free to campaign at home, in New York which had become the major goal of the suffrage forces. As the richest, most populous state in the Union, New York had the greatest number of Representatives. A victory in the

Empire State might create enough favorable pressure to force adoption of a federal amendment.

The main obstacle to this aim was the borough of Manhattan, with its enormous immigrant vote and its powerful Tammany Hall, long a foe of woman suffrage.

Carrie headed the New York campaign. Pondering the strategy of her greatest adversary, the Tammany machine, she had one of those inspirations which made her so formidable as an opponent. The strength of Tammany Hall lay in its widespread, skillfully controlled organization, which, to date, had defeated every political group. She decided it was high time women created a machine of their own, patterned after the Tammany system. They would call it "The Woman's Party." Its birth was hailed by political observers as an astute move. Women were learning the game too thoroughly for comfort. For the first time suffragists were reckoned as a "political force."

Carrie was in the full swing of the New York campaign, the most brilliantly planned and executed in suffrage history, when Anna Howard Shaw, sensing the accelerated pace of the fight, and knowing herself physically unequal to the coming strains, resigned her Presidency of the National Association.

Over Carrie's own protest, and over that of New York suffragists, who saw their chief snatched from them at a crucial moment in their campaign, the Association nominated her to fill the vacancy. Carrie refused. The Association then tried another maneuver. The annual convention was being held in Washington. At a moment when it was known Carrie was absent from her hotel room, delegates from every state filed in quietly. When she returned she faced a silent and determined crowd. The demonstration meant only one thing. The National Association would nominate no one else.

The realization stunned Carrie. The last thing she had expected or desired was to be recalled to the Presidency. Ten years ago her term of office had encountered its share of factions, rivalries, resistance. To assume leadership now, when the struggle for the franchise was rapidly reaching a climax, was to accept overwhelming responsibilities and burdens.

She had given her youth to the Cause. She had planned and directed immense undertakings with scarcely a pause, and now came this call to renewed effort, the greatest yet demanded of her.

"I'm old, I'm no longer healthy and I'm tired," she summed up her present qualifications to the waiting delegates. Then, with a dry little smile and a shrug, she yielded. "I'll do my best."

They smiled back at her, wonderfully relieved, and not a little amused at her estimate of herself at fifty-six.

Her hair was gray, and shadows showed under her eyes, but time had added to, not diminished, her stature. A widely traveled citizen of the world, she was rich in her understanding of people and nations, and a skilled diplomat. Her smile could be full of charm, but a streak of amused cynicism underlay her humor and made her wit pungent. Forcefulness had replaced the driving energy of her youth. Experience had deepened her authority. She was at the height of her powers.

She needed all her gift for strong leadership and all the political wisdom she had acquired to steer the Movement through the next five arduous years. In 1917, New York granted suffrage to its women, and now the final push for the Federal Amendment started.

But that year also marked the entry of the United States in the war. As always in times of war, public emotions were tense and domestic issues subordinate to the all-important one of winning the conflict. Meanwhile the situation in the suffrage arena had become complex. Another rift was imminent. A militant party had sprung up led by Alice Paul, a young American Quaker, who, while engaged in social work in England, had become a devoted adherent of Emmeline Pankhurst.

On her return to the States, Alice Paul joined the fight for woman suffrage in America. Her ardent convictions made her contribution a forceful one, but it was soon apparent that her methods of crusading and those of the National American Association were opposed. The Association refused to embarrass or put undue pressure on the administration during a national conflict. Miss Paul was dedicated to the strategy she had seen used with success in England. She therefore separated herself from the main body of suffragists affiliated with Carrie, and with a following of her own, established an independent "Woman's Party" in Washington. Once more, and at the most crucial moment in its history, the Woman's Rights Movement was divided.

But inner conflict could not destroy the gains already made. In the main, the friends of the Cause in Congress remained loyal throughout the war years, and President Wilson was a sympathetic ally. In June of the year 1919, the Sixty-Sixth Congress passed the Nineteenth Amendment. President Wilson, in Paris at the time, and harassed by the tragic failure of his plans for a just peace, took time to send American women a cablegram of congratulations. Englishwomen, who had won the vote earlier, cabled two words: "GLORY HALLE-LUJAH!" All over the world the news flashed. The National Association Headquarters were swamped with telegrams of rejoicing.

But the victory was not yet certain. Thirty-six states out of forty-eight had to ratify the amendment before it could become law. Eleven sent in their approval almost immediately. Carrie did not wait for the rest. She launched a ratification campaign all over the country.

TWELVE

On an August day in 1920, a year and two months after the amendment had received Congressional approval, Carrie, travel-weary and worn to the point of exhaustion, sat with two of her aides in a room of the National American Headquarters in Washington. After the most grilling fight of her entire experience, ratification had finally been achieved in Tennessee, last state to hold out against the amendment.

The three were watching and waiting for a message from the Secretary of State, officially confirming the enfranchisement of twenty-seven million women.

It was summer. Open windows in the room admitted a suffocating warmth, but the humid temperature was a mild parallel to the heat of violent controversy and insane opposition from which they had emerged in Tennessee.

When at last the curt, sharp summons of the telephone broke the quiet, Carrie drew a deep breath and rose slowly to answer it. The other two stiffened, their eyes fixed on their leader. By the sudden relaxing of her tired body as she hung up the instrument, and her long, wordless look of triumph, they knew the fight was ended.

In that moment of silence, thirty-three years of slow and often heartbreaking struggle receded for Carrie like a dream.

Next morning, an exultant multitude packed the Pennsylvania Station in New York City, awaiting the arrival of a train an hour overdue from Washington. For the most part they were women who made up that restless, impatient crowd. Apart from the throng stood a reception committee of distinguished citizens—Governor Smith with his staff in full military regalia, and a special delegation with banners and flowers.

At last a flurry was noticeable by the closed train gate. It slid open with a metallic rattle. The mass of expectant watchers strained to attention.

"Here she comes!" shrilled a voice, and the place broke into pandemonium.

They cheered as women may never cheer again—wildly, hysterically, and above that high, triumphing note from hundreds of throats rose the crashing strains of *Hail the Conquering Hero Comes,* by New York's Seventy-First Regiment band.

Before the impact of her tremendous welcome, Carrie stood bewildered. Through the din she became aware that someone had thrust an immense bunch of delphiniums and chrysanthemums into her arms.

Hat off and hand extended, Governor Smith was congratulating her. The jam of milling, shouting people pressed closer. Then, hardly knowing how she got there, she was in an open automobile, confronting another delirious crowd outside.

Fatigue and confusion were swept away in a rush of exhilaration. Standing erect, she answered with upflung arm the deafening ovation that continued all the way along Thirty-Fourth Street. The old Waldorf-Astoria and its great ballroom were as packed as the sidewalks. Police guards pushed a path for her through the mob.

Finally, when some semblance of order was restored, and the room settled down to listen, she spoke to an enthralled audience, describing the last grim phase in her battle in Tennessee for the winning of a great freedom. And while she talked, in all the major cities of the United States bells were ringing and whistles blowing a paean of victory.

The seventy-two-year war for full citizenship was won in America, but Carrie foresaw dangers as well as opportunities for women now they held the powerful weapon of the franchise. The temptation to disband and lose interest when the goal was reached was inevitable. Instead of dissolving the suffrage organization with its great army of intelligently trained workers, why not let it continue to operate for a different purpose and under a different name? Women were going to need a bureau of bipartisan political information in order to use the vote to the best advantage. Thus came into being the League of Women Voters, which has remained ever since a vital force for good citizenship.

The International Woman Suffrage Alliance meanwhile was staging a slow revival in Europe after the war. Carrie was still its President. There was much the Alliance could do to heal the aftermath of bitterness left by the conflict. Deeply troubled by her country's refusal to participate in world affairs, she rallied women in support of the League of Nations. With many thoughtful people she watched the growing racial hatreds, the economic rivalries and vaulting ambitions of

European leaders, which she knew were heading the world toward fresh disaster. Never a passive observer, she launched into a new crusade to find the cause and cure of war.

Perhaps the deepest discouragement she was ever to know came with advancing years, as she realized the futility of her efforts for peace and saw the nations swept into a second cataclysm. After that, and until her death in 1947 at the age of eighty-eight, Mrs. Catt remained in active retirement, a keen observer of international events, venerated by a large following and still dedicated to promoting the welfare of women and the brotherhood of nations.

Men and women who see the democratic way of life endangered today need her ringing reminder given at the time the franchise was won:

"The vote is the emblem of your equality, the guarantee of your liberty . . . the vote is a power, a weapon of offense and defense, a prayer. Understand what it means and what it can do for your country. Use it intelligently, conscientiously, prayerfully."

Looking back over the years, one can see how logically and inevitably the idea of an emancipated womanhood grew in the democratic soil of the New World. It took root as early as 1701, on an island where independent thought and action were thrust on women, and where Quaker teachings raised them to a place of equality with the other half of the human race. The Nantucket way of life was a sturdy, fearless heritage. While it lasted it produced remarkable women.

The names of Mary Coffin Starbuck (the "Great Woman" of the early settlement), Abiah Folger, mother of Benjamin Franklin, Lucretia Mott, called "the most enlightened woman of her day," and Maria Mitchell, America's first woman astronomer, belong to history.

Lucretia carried her Nantucket heritage to the mainland, where, under her influence, the idea of women's equality gathered adherents. Its momentum raised a great disturbance and the dust has not yet entirely settled. Even now, the lives of Lucretia Mott, Elizabeth Cady Stanton, Lucy Stone, Susan B. Anthony and Carrie Chapman Catt are so forceful a challenge they still stir resentment in certain quarters.

They were accused in their day of being embittered, disappointed wives and spinsters, who vented their spleen on the male sex and sought compensation in notoriety. Recently, in more clinical language, modern psychiatry has concurred.

The facts paint a different picture. Lucretia, Elizabeth, Lucy, and Carrie were gifted and well-adjusted women, all of them happily married to men who matched them in brains and courage. Susan alone chose spinsterhood, a fact which did not deprive her of a wide and stimulating association with men, on a more equal footing than any woman of her time. Susan, the most brutally caricatured of the five, is enshrined now, with seventy-five of her fellow-countrymen in the Hall of Fame. The bronze tablet that bears her name summarizes in her own words what she thought on the subject of sex.

"The day will come when man will recognize woman as his peer, not only at the fireside but in the councils of the nation. Then . . . will there be the perfect comradeship . . . between the sexes that shall result in the highest development of the race."
Susan B. Anthony from an address, June 27, 1899.

The movement started at Seneca Falls in a remote little village church had a lasting impact. Startling developments have occurred since then. First the machine and then the atomic age have brought to light undreamed-of possibilities and perils. But all during that time a new woman has been evolving, as if in preparation for the crisis. Who will say that her advance, impelled by these five leaders, is not one of the significant events of the fateful Twentieth Century?

BIBLIOGRAPHY

_____*Our Famous Women. By twenty eminent authors.* An authorized record of the lives and deeds of distinguished American women of our time, Hartford: A. D. Worthington and Company, 1884.

AUSTIN, GEORGE LOWELL. *The Life and Times of Wendell Phillips.* Boston: B. B. Russell & Company, 1884.

BIRNEY, CATHERINE H. *The Grimké Sisters, Sarah and Angelina Grimké,* the first American women advocates of abolition and woman's rights. Boston: Lee & Shepard, 1885.

BLACKWELL, ALICE STONE. *Lucy Stone: Pioneer of Woman's Rights.* Boston: Little, Brown & Co., 1930. $3.00.

BLOOMER, DEXTER CHAMBERLAIN. *Life and Writings of Amelia Bloomer.* Boston: Arena Publishing Co., 1895.

CATT, CARRIE CHAPMAN, and SHULER, NETTIE ROGERS, *Woman Suffrage and Politics.* The inner story of the suffrage movement. New York: Charles Scribner's Sons, 1923.

CHILD, LYDIA MARIE (FRANCIS). *Brief History of the Condition of Women, in Various Ages and Nations.* (2 v., 5th ed.) New York and Boston: C. S. Francis and Company, 1854.

CREVECOEUR, DE MICHAEL GUILLAUME ST. JOHN. *Letters from an American Farmer.* Philadelphia. From the press of Mathew Carey, March 4, 1793.

DORR, RHETA LOUISE (CHILDE). *Susan B. Anthony: The Woman Who Changed the Mind of a Nation.* New York: Frederick A. Stokes Company, 1928. $5.00.

GARRISON, WENDELL PHILLIPS, and GARRISON, F. J. *William Lloyd Garrison: The Story of His Life Told by His Children.* Boston and New York: Houghton Mifflin and Company, 1894.

GODFREY, EDWARD K. *The Island of Nantucket.* Boston: Lee and Shepard, 1882.

GODWIN, MARY WOLLESTONECRAFT. *A Vindication of Rights of Woman,* 1792.

HALLOWELL, ANNA DAVIS. *James and Lucretia Mott: Life and Letters.* Edited by their granddaughter. Boston: Printed by Peter Edes for Thomas and Andrews, 1884.

HARPER, IDA HUSTED. *The Life and Work of Susan B. Anthony.* Indianapolis: The Bowen-Merrill Company, 1899-1908.

HIGGINSON, MARY POTTER (THACHER). *Thomas Wentworth Higginson.* Boston and New York: Houghton Mifflin Company, 1914.

LUTZ, ALMA, *Created Equal: A Biography of Elizabeth Cary Stanton,* New York: The John Day Company, 1940. $3.75.

MACY, OBED. *The History of Nantucket.* Boston: Hilliard, Gray and Company, 1835.

MACY, WILLIAM FRANCIS. *The Story of Old Nantucket.* (2nd rev. and enl. ed.) Boston: Houghton Mifflin Co., 1928. $1.50.

ROUSSEAU, JEAN-JACQUES. *Emile: Treatise on Education.*

STANTON, ELIZABETH CADY. *Eighty Years and More.* New York: European Publishing Company, 1898.

——————————*The Woman's Bible.* (2 v.) New York: European Publishing Company, 1895-1898.

STANTON, THEODORE and BLATCH, HARRIOT STANTON (EDITORS). *Elizabeth Cady Stanton as Revealed in Her Letters, Diary and Reminiscences.* New York and London: Harper & Brothers, 1922.

STEVENS, WILLIAM OLIVER. *Nantucket, the Far-Away Island.* New York: Dodd, Mead & Company, 1936. $3.50.

[*Note:* All these titles, except *Created Equal* and *Nantucket, the Far-Away Island,* are out of print.]

Collections

Papers, letters, manuscripts, clippings (Elizabeth Cady Stanton.) Washington, D.C.: Library of Congress.

Scrapbook of clippings related to Elizabeth Cady Stanton, collected by Susan B. Anthony. Washington, D.C.: Library of Congress.

Woman's Rights Collection. Cambridge, Mass.: Radcliffe College.

Newspapers

The Lily. New York: New York Public Library.

The Revolution, Vols. 1-5. New York: New York Public Library.

Periodicals

Eminent Women of the Age. Hartford, Conn.: S. M. Betts Co., 1895.